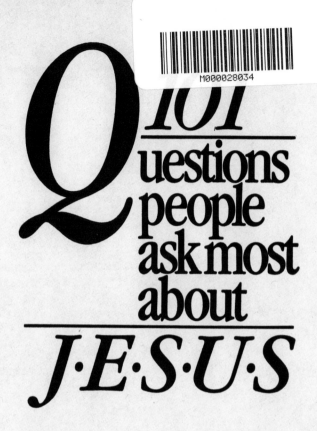

Q 101 Questions people ask most about J·E·S·U·S

DON STEWART

Tyndale House Publishers, Inc.
Wheaton, Illinois

All Scripture is taken from the
New King James Version unless
otherwise noted.

Third printing, June 1989

Library of Congress Catalog Card Number 86-50995
ISBN 0-8423-4748-8
Copyright 1986 by Don Stewart
All rights reserved
Printed in the United States of America

101 Questions
People Ask Most about Jesus

Contents

Part II Jesus: His Nature

Conclusion to Part II

Part III Jesus: His Deeds

Conclusion to Part III

Part IV   Jesus: His Importance to You and Me

Part I

Jesus: His Existence

He is the Ancient Wisdom of the World,
The Word Creative, Beautiful and True,
The Nameless of Innumerable Names,
Ageless Forever, yet Forever New.
Charles Carroll Albertson
The Holy Child

And the Word became flesh and dwelt among us,
and we beheld His glory, the glory as of
the only begotten of the Father, full of grace and truth.
—John 1:14

This first section will cover questions about the existence of Jesus and the reliability of the records about him. We will answer such questions as: Did Jesus exist? What sources are there that give us information concerning him? Is the New Testament a reliable source of information about Jesus? Can it be trusted to convey an accurate picture of his life and ministry? Has the text of the New Testament been changed as it has been transmitted down throughout history?

1. Is It Important to Examine the Life of Jesus?

Before we answer any questions about the meaning of the life of Jesus Christ we need to answer one preliminary question. Why? Why is it important to consider the life of Jesus Christ? Granted, he is an important historical figure, but what makes him so special?

The reason that it is important to look at the life of Jesus goes beyond historical curiosity, for it is a matter of the highest importance. When Jesus came to earth, he claimed that the eternal destiny of every man, woman, and child would depend upon how they viewed him. If his claims are true, the decision we make about Jesus will determine whether we spend eternity with him or without him. Nothing could be more important.

The message of the Bible can be summed up as follows: In the beginning an all-powerful, personal God created the heavens and the earth. In his final act of creation God created man and woman. God put them in a perfect environment giving them everything they needed for their happiness. But the man and woman sinned against God, disobeying the only commandment he had given them. Their disobedience led to a

13

separation between them and God. They were banished from the Paradise that God had provided for them.

But God did not want it to stay that way. He promised that he would take care of the sin that separated humanity from him. The Old Testament contains a number of promises that a Savior, or Messiah, would come and solve the sin problem.

The New Testament opens with the birth of this Promised One. His name is Jesus, which means "Yahweh is my salvation." He is also given the title Christ, which means "the Messiah."

Some thirty years after Jesus' birth, a rugged individual named John the Baptist appeared in the Judean desert announcing the soon appearance of the promised Messiah. When Jesus arrived at the Jordan River where John was baptizing, he was identified as the "Lamb of God," the one who would take away the sins of the world. After he was baptized, Jesus was tempted for forty days in the wilderness by the Devil. Once his temptation was complete, the sinless Jesus began his public ministry.

Jesus' public ministry lasted some three short years, but in that time he lived a life such as no one has lived before or since. He did things that no one else has ever done. He healed the lame, the blind, the deaf, the mute, and caused a storm to immediately cease. His friend Lazarus was four days dead but Jesus brought him back to life. The people of his day, upon seeing the miracles which Jesus did, testified, "We never saw anything like this!" (Mark 2:12).

Jesus also said things such as no one else has ever said. After finishing his Sermon on the Mount, the Scripture records that the people were astonished at his teaching. He spoke to them as one who had authority. Jesus claimed authority: authority over disease, authority over nature, authority over the supernatural, and authority over life and death. He claimed to be the one who had the power to forgive sins, to raise the dead on Judgment Day and to grant eternal life to whoever believed in him.

He was betrayed by one of his own disciples and crucified

under the Roman governor, Pontius Pilate. Yet the New Testament records that three days later he appeared to Peter— and to others—alive. He had risen from the dead just as he said he would. By doing this, Jesus demonstrated the truth of his claims. The Bible says Jesus' death on the cross was for the sins of the world. His death has made it possible for mankind to be back in relationship with God. One must believe in Jesus and accept his sacrifice on their behalf to have forgiveness of sins and life everlasting.

The Bible also says that Jesus will return again someday. Those who believe in him will enjoy everlasting life; those who do not believe in him will spend eternity apart from God.

As you can see, Jesus Christ's identity is of utmost importance. It is crucial that we consider him and see if he is the one whom he made himself out to be. If he is the eternal God who became man, then what we decide about him will determine our eternal destiny. There is no issue more important.

2. How Do We Know That Jesus Existed?

Did a person named Jesus of Nazareth exist? Before we can answer questions on the life and ministry of Jesus, we must first establish the fact of his existence. This is not difficult to do, for both friend and foe alike testify that the man, Jesus, did exist.

The New Testament consists of twenty-seven separate documents which were written by people living in the first century who had personal contact with Jesus. All of these writings testify to the existence of Jesus. These New Testament witnesses can be divided as follows: the four Gospels, the Book of Acts, the letters of Paul, and the universal letters.

The four Gospels. The four Gospels, Matthew, Mark, Luke, and John, each give an account of the life of Jesus. Matthew and John were two of Jesus' twelve disciples. They wrote with firsthand knowledge of what Jesus said and did. Mark wrote

15

about the life of Jesus from the viewpoint of Simon Peter, who was one of the twelve. Luke wrote from the perspective of Jesus' mother, Mary. He asserted that his account was based upon the testimony of eyewitnesses. Therefore, we have four independent writings, each of them recording eyewitness testimony to the fact that Jesus did exist.

The Book of Acts. The Book of Acts, written by Luke, records the birth and rise of the New Testament church. After Jesus came back from the dead, he gave his disciples instructions on how to proclaim his message. The Book of Acts records the struggles of his disciples to do this. Their experiences and preaching give further testimony to Jesus' existence.

The letters of Paul. The thirteen letters of Paul make up a large part of the New Testament. Paul, formerly named Saul, was a devout Jew who hated Christians to the point that he put them in jail and consented to their execution. Yet one day when he was on the road to Damascus to persecute Christians, Jesus spoke to him. This resulted in Saul's conversion. The remainder of his life was spent spreading the gospel of Jesus Christ. Paul's letters give convincing testimony to Jesus' existence.

The universal letters. The remainder of the New Testament consists of letters by certain disciples of Jesus. We have two from Simon Peter (1 and 2 Peter), one from James, one from Jude, four from John (1, 2, 3 John and the Book of Revelation) and the anonymous letter to the Hebrews. These writings contain instruction and encouragement to the believers in Jesus. They give firsthand testimony to the fact of Jesus' life and ministry.

Finally, there is the testimony of Jesus' enemies, the Jews and Romans. They did not endorse the ministry of Jesus and tried— without success—to stop Christianity from growing. In all their efforts, however, we never find them denying Jesus' existence. They attempted to make him out as a deceiver and blasphemer, and by doing so, admitted that he existed.

Therefore, the question of the existence of Jesus is not an issue. Twenty-seven separate documents written by people who had personal contact with Jesus testify to the fact that he did indeed exist. We add to their testimony that of the Jews and the Romans. Neither of these groups believed in Jesus and they tried everything that they could to stop Christianity from growing. Yet they never denied that he existed.

Thus we can confidently say that the issue of Jesus' existence is not an issue at all. Every source, friendly and unfriendly, testified that he existed.

3. Could the New Testament Account of Jesus Be Just an Exaggeration?

The story of Jesus as recorded in the New Testament is miraculous. From his birth through his resurrection, Jesus is portrayed as someone who is from heaven. He is the eternal God who came down to earth and became a human being. We have already demonstrated that the existence of Jesus is beyond question. Granted that he did exist, could the New Testament story of Jesus be only a legend? Is it possible that what we have in the New Testament is a fabrication or exaggeration of what occurred?

There are several problems with this view. First is the testimony of his disciples. They contended that Jesus did these miraculous deeds in their presence. The Apostle John wrote, "And he who has seen has testified, and his testimony is true; and he knows that he is telling the truth, so that you may believe" (John 19:35). Simon Peter made it clear that the disciples knew the difference between myth and reality. "For we did not follow cunningly devised fables when we made known to you the power and coming of our Lord Jesus Christ, but were eyewitnesses of His majesty" (2 Pet. 1:16). It is the united testimony of the New Testament that Jesus performed miracles in front of multitudes of people.

These same disciples are the ones who gave us the New

17

Testament record. The Gospel writers, Matthew and John, were disciples of Jesus and eyewitnesses to the events. Mark and Luke recorded eyewitness testimony. Thus, we have individuals who were with Jesus and witnessed these events firsthand. They are not passing down a story to us that they had been told. They were there!

Furthermore, these same disciples are united in their portrait of Jesus. From the first statement until the last, everything that they record about Jesus testifies to his supernatural ability.

Finally, if the New Testament account of Jesus were merely an invention or exaggeration, then why didn't his enemies say so? Those who hated Christ would have denied his miracles if they could have. Yet they attempted to explain his miraculous character by attributing his works to the power of Satan. Rather than deny that Jesus was a miracle worker, his enemies tried to say his power was demonic.

Thus, to say the New Testament portrait of Jesus was an invention or exaggeration does not fit the facts. Instead:

1. The testimony we have from the New Testament is from firsthand sources. The disciples recorded what they heard and saw.
2. The New Testament testimony is consistent. Jesus is pictured as supernatural from the beginning of his life to the end.
3. The enemies of Jesus also testify to his supernatural abilities. Instead of denying his miracles, they argued that Jesus' power was not from God but from Satan.

4. What Is the Purpose of the Four Gospels?

The only firsthand testimony that we have about the life and teachings of Jesus come from the four Gospels. It is important that we understand these sources and what they are trying to accomplish. The Gospels are neither biographies of the life of Christ nor are they a disinterested record of certain events in his life. Each writer wants you to know the truth about Jesus and to become a disciple. To accomplish this purpose, each

Gospel is aimed at a certain audience and each writer is selective of the events he includes.

Matthew. The Gospel according to Matthew is aimed primarily at the Jew, the person familiar with the Old Testament. Jesus is portrayed as Israel's Messiah, the King of the Jews. Matthew records how the promises God made in the Old Testament with regard to the Messiah are fulfilled in Jesus.

Matthew begins his book by stating the family tree of Jesus. "The book of the genealogy of Jesus Christ, the Son of David, the Son of Abraham" (Matt. 1:1). This genealogy demonstrates that Jesus is the rightful heir to the kingdom that was promised to David and his descendants and sets the tone for the book. The remainder of the book emphasizes that Jesus has the credentials to be Israel's Messiah.

Mark. Mark, on the other hand, is not writing to the Jew or to those who are familiar with the Old Testament. His audience is basically those people in the Roman Empire who are unfamiliar with the religion of the Jews. Consequently, Mark's Gospel does not start with the birth of Jesus or any family tree that demonstrates Jesus as a fulfillment of prophecy. It starts, rather, with the beginning of Jesus' ministry. "The beginning of the gospel of Jesus Christ, the Son of God" (Mark 1:1). Mark's is a Gospel of action. Jesus is portrayed as the servant of the Lord doing the job that God has sent him to do. Thus, the emphasis is on doing, and Mark shows that Jesus got the job done.

Luke. Luke was written to those more intellectually minded. He states his purpose in the book's prologue: "Inasmuch as many have taken in hand to set in order a narrative of those things which are most surely believed among us, just as those who from the beginning were eyewitnesses and ministers of the word delivered them to us, it seemed good to me also, having had perfect understanding of all things from the very first, to write to you an orderly account" (Luke 1:1-3). Luke is not writing as an eyewitness but as one who is recording the eyewitness testimony. His portrayal of Jesus is as the perfect man. Hence, he focuses on those events in Jesus' life that stress his humanity. The Greeks in their art and literature were always looking for the perfect man. The Gospel of Luke reveals that man.

John. John emphasizes that Jesus was God. John was an eyewitness to the life of Jesus and the things he recorded were for the purpose of establishing the fact that Jesus was God. John wanted his readers to exercise faith toward Jesus. "And truly Jesus did many other signs in the presence of His disciples, which are not written in this book; but these are written that you may believe that Jesus is the Christ, the Son of God, and that believing you may have life in His name" (John 20:30, 31). When John states his purpose he also states that he is selective in what he has recorded.

Therefore, we can say the following about the four Gospels:
1. They are not intended to be a history or biography of the life of Christ in the modern sense of the term. Each author is selective in what he portrays. Jesus did many more things than the Gospels record, as John testified, "And there are also many other things that Jesus did, which if they were written one by one, I suppose that even the world itself could not contain the books that would be written" (John 21:25).
2. Each author is presenting a different aspect of Jesus' character. In Matthew, Jesus is the king; in Mark, he is the servant; in Luke, he is the perfect man; in John, he is God. This is because each writer addressed a different type of audience.
3. When the Gospels are compared with each other, we get an overall portrait of Jesus. He was God from all eternity who came down to earth as the perfect man. He was the Messiah of Israel, the King of the Jews, the one who did the job that

God had sent Him to do. This is the testimony of the four Gospels.

5. What Prompted the Gospels to Be Written?

As already stated, the account of the life of Jesus recorded in the four Gospels was written either by those who were eyewitnesses to the events or by those who recorded eyewitness testimony. Although there is nothing directly stated as to why the life of Jesus was committed to writing, there are seemingly two obvious answers.

The primary reason the Gospels were written was for the benefit of future generations. After the events occurred and were observed by eyewitnesses, they were proclaimed among the people. Rather than have the story transmitted orally from generation to generation, those who were intimately involved in the life of Jesus decided to write down what had occurred. This way, those living after them would have their eyewitness testimony before them and could be certain of what really happened in the life of Jesus.

A second reason for the writing of the Gospels concerns keeping the truth of the story intact. The testimony of the disciples who observed Jesus' life and teachings was recorded to prevent people from accidentally or deliberately changing the story. Committing the story of Jesus to writing made it very difficult for someone to come on the scene later and say Jesus didn't say this or didn't do that. Immediately, the record could be checked. If someone attempted to bring a different story, he would have to present credentials that were as good as or better than the four Gospels.

Because we have the testimony of those who were there, we can have confidence in the record which they gave to us. We also need not worry about someone new coming on the scene with a different account, for only those who participated in the events have a right to tell us what happened. As the Gospel writers testify, the things they recorded are what they saw and heard, as in the case of Matthew and John; or the writing of eyewitness testimony, as is true of Mark and Luke.

6. Did Jesus Aid the Disciples in Remembering His Teachings?

The New Testament does not give us any specific reasons why the life of Jesus was committed to writing. However, it does anticipate this happening. On the night of Jesus' betrayal he promised his disciples that they would remember what he had taught them.

While they were together in the upper room, Jesus told his disciples he was going away but that he would not leave them alone. He promised to send the Holy Spirit to be with them: "Nevertheless I tell you the truth. It is to your advantage that I go away; for if I do not go away, the Helper will not come to you; but if I depart, I will send Him to you" (John 16:7). The Holy Spirit, or the Helper, would be with them as Jesus was with them.

Among the things the Holy Spirit would do was bring back Jesus' teachings to their remembrance. "But the Helper, the Holy Spirit, whom the Father will send in My name, He will teach you all things, and bring to your remembrance all things that I said to you" (John 14:26). This promise that Jesus gave his disciples was one of total recall. The Holy Spirit supernaturally aided the disciples in remembering all things that Jesus said. This is important when we consider the fact that these same disciples either wrote the Gospels or were directly involved in their composition. They were the ones who gave the world the firsthand story of Jesus.

Jesus went on to say of the Holy Spirit, "He will guide you into all truth" (John 16:13). This is another testimony to the fact that these disciples would tell the truth about Jesus because of the guidance of the Holy Spirit.

How did Jesus aid the disciples in remembering his teachings?

1. The New Testament testifies that Jesus promised his disciples the Holy Spirit as their Helper.
2. One of the ministries of the Holy Spirit was to bring back to the disciples accurate remembrances of those things Jesus said and did.
3. These same disciples are the ones who gave the world the firsthand written account of Jesus as recorded in the four Gospels. This being the case, we have the testimony of Jesus that those things written in the four Gospels were accurate in all that they said.

7. What Do Sources, Apart from the New Testament, Say about Jesus?

There are numerous sources, other than the New Testament, that mention Jesus. These writings are recognized as secondary sources because they are not based on firsthand knowledge of the events of the life of Christ. Nevertheless, these sources are valuable because they:

1. testify to Jesus' existence; and
2. confirm the basic record of Jesus' life as recorded in the New Testament.

Flavius Josephus (A.D. 37-100). Apart from the New Testament, the earliest testimony of Jesus that has survived is from the Jewish writer, Flavius Josephus. He had this to say: "Now there was about this time, Jesus, a wise man, if it be lawful to call him a man, for he was a doer of wonderful works—a teacher of such men as receive the truth with pleasure. He drew over to him both many of the Jews, and many of the Gentiles.

"He was Christ; and when Pilate, at the suggestion of the principal men amongst us, had condemned him to the cross, those who loved him at the first did not forsake him, for he appeared to them alive again the third day, as the divine prophets had foretold these and ten thousand other wonderful things concerning him; and the tribe of Christians, so named from him, are not extinct at this day" *(Antiquites, XVIII, III)*.

The complete trustworthiness of this passage has been called into question because it refers to Jesus as the Messiah (the Christ). Whether entirely authentic or not, the passage gives testimony to Jesus' existence.

Thallus (c. A.D. 52). Thallus was a Samaritan-born historian whose writings have not survived to the present day. Another writer, however—Julius Africanus (A.D. 221)—cites the writings of Thallus saying that Thallus attempted to explain away the three-hour period of darkness at the time of Christ's crucifixion: "Thallus, in the third book of his histories, explains away this darkness as an eclipse of the sun— unreasonable, as it seems to me."

In attempting to explain the three-hour period of darkness, Thallus gives testimony that such an event did occur. His nonsupernatural explanation of the event is impossible because Christ died at the time of Passover when there was a full moon; and a solar eclipse cannot take place at the time of a full moon. We are indebted to Julius Africanus for this glimpse into the writings of Thallus.

The Letter of Mara Bar-Serapion (after A.D. 73). In the British Museum there is a letter written during the first century A.D. by a father to his son in prison. The father compares the deaths of Socrates, Pythagoras, and Jesus. "What advantage did the Jews gain from executing their wise King? It was just after that that their kingdom was abolished. . . . But Socrates did not die for good; he lived on in the teaching of Plato. Pythagoras did not die for good; he lived on in the statue of Hera. Nor did the wise King die for good; he lived on in the teaching which he had given."

Cornelius Tacitus (early second century). Cornelius Tacitus, a Roman historian living in the early second century, wrote about the reign of Caesar Nero. Tacitus records that Nero shifted the blame for the burning of Rome from himself to the Christians. "Hence to suppress the rumor, he falsely charged with guilt, and punished with the most exquisite tortures, the persons commonly called Christians, who were hated for their enormities. Christus, the founder of the name was put to death by Pontius Pilate, procurator of Judea in the reign of Tiberius: not only through Judea, where the mischief originated, but through the city of Rome also" *(Annals, XV, 44)*. He also refers to Christianity in another section of his *Histories* when speaking of the burning of the temple and the manuscripts of Tacitus' *Histories*. We know about this reference from another writer, Sulpicius Serverus *(Chronicles, 30.6)*, who preserved the reference from Tacitus.

Pliny the Younger (c. A.D. 112). Pliny the Younger was governor of Bithynia. He wrote a letter to the Emperor Trajan saying that he had killed numerous Christians. He also had this to say of the Christians: "They were in the habit of meeting on a certain fixed day before it was light, when they sang in alternate verse a hymn to Christ as to a god, and bound themselves to the solemn oath, not to do any wicked deeds, and never to deny a truth when they should be called upon to deliver it up" *(Epistles, X, 96)*.

Suetonius (c. A.D. 120). Suetonius was a court official under the Emperor Hadrian. He wrote of Claudius Caesar: "As the Jews were making constant disturbances at the instigation of Chestus [an alternative spelling of Christ] he expelled them from Rome" *(Life of Cladius, 25.4)*. Suetonius also wrote, "Punishment by Nero was inflicted on the Christians, a class of men given to a new and mischievous superstition" *(Lives of the Caesars, 26.2)*.

Lucian (second century). The Greek satirist Lucian alluded to Jesus, ". . . the man who was crucified in Palestine because he introduced this new cult into the world. . . .

Furthermore, their first lawgiver persuaded them that they were all brothers one of another after they have transgressed once for all by denying the Greek gods and by worshiping that crucified sophist himself and living under his laws" *(On the Death of Peregrine).*

The Talmud. The Talmud is a collection of Jewish writings constituting the religious and civil law. They were completed by A.D. 500. The Talmud states: "On the eve of Passover they hanged Yeshu (of Nazareth) and the herald went before him for forty days saying (Yeshu of Nazareth) is going to be stoned in that he hath practiced sorcery and beguiled and led astray Israel. Let everyone know aught in his defense come and plead for him. But they found naught in his defense and hanged him on the eve of Passover" *(The Babylonian Talmud, Sanhedrin 43a, "Eve of Passover").*

The Talmud contains a further reference to Jesus: "I found a genealogical roll in Jerusalem wherein was recorded, Such-an-one is a bastard of an adulteress" *(R. Shimeon ben' Azzai Yeb, IV, 3.49a).*

Both of these references corroborate the New Testament picture of how unbelievers viewed Jesus. They accused him of being demon-possessed. "But when the Pharisees heard it they said, 'This fellow does not cast out demons except by Beelzebub, the ruler of the demons' (Matthew 12:24). They also accused him of being an illegitimate child. "We were not born of fornication" (John 8:41).

These are the early references, apart from the New Testament, to Jesus Christ and his followers. As we can readily see, the references are limited and are not of a firsthand nature. They are extremely valuable, however, in that they corroborate the basic outline of the life of Jesus as given in the New Testament and give further testimony to the accuracy of the New Testament record. These secondary sources testify that:
1. There was controversy concerning the birth of Christ. Those

who did not believe him to be virgin born concluded he
was an illegitimate child.

2. The religious leaders believed Jesus' miraculous deeds were
   due to him being demon-possessed.

3. Jesus was crucified during the Passover when Pontius Pilate
   was governor of Judea.

4. There were three hours of unexplained darkness at his
   crucifixion.

5. His disciples believed that Jesus had risen from the dead.

6. The early Christians worshiped Christ as God.

7. Christianity spread to Rome at an early date.

8. The early Christians were persecuted by the Roman
   emperors.

8. How Soon after the Life of Jesus Was the New Testament Written?

A crucial question to be considered is the length of time
between the life and ministry of Jesus and the composition of
the New Testament. Was there a long interval between his life
and the writing of the New Testament? Can we trust what the
New Testament says?

We are fortunate that the New Testament was written down in
a relatively short time after the life and ministry of Jesus. After
Jesus' ascension into heaven, the disciples spread his message
orally. Before they died, however, the books of the New
Testament were written, giving us an eyewitness account of
what transpired.

From the internal evidence provided by the New Testament
we know that the Gospels were written at an early date. The
Book of Acts records the birth of the church and its early
missionary activity and it concludes with the Apostle Paul
arriving in Rome. Nothing is mentioned of his death. Since
Paul's life and ministry are the central theme of the latter half
of the Book of Acts, this leads us to believe that the book was
composed while he was still alive.

If Paul were still alive when the Book of Acts was completed, it is of the utmost significance. Paul died in the Neronian persecution around A.D. 64. That would mean the Book of Acts was written prior to that time. Now the Book of Acts was *sequel* to the Gospel according to Luke. Therefore, Luke would have to have been composed some time before Acts, probably in the late fifties of the first century. The death of Christ occurred around A.D. 30. Therefore, we are talking of a time span of less than thirty years between Christ's death and the writing of Luke's Gospel.

Furthermore, the general teaching of the early church was that Matthew was the first Gospel written. If this is the case, then we are even closer to the events at hand.

There is another reason to believe that the Gospels were written at an early date. The first three Gospels, Matthew, Mark, and Luke, were written before the city of Jerusalem was destroyed. Each of them has Jesus predicting the destruction of the city and none of them give any indication that the city had been destroyed. The city of Jerusalem was destroyed in A.D. 70, so we must assume that these three Gospels were written before that time.

If the early date of the Gospels is accurate, as the evidence leads us to believe, it means the life and deeds of Jesus were written and circulated at a time when other eyewitnesses, apart from the apostles, could evaluate what they said. It must be remembered that there were many unfriendly eyewitnesses to Jesus' ministry. Some of these individuals would still have been alive when the Gospels were written and circulated. If the writers had exaggerated or distorted the facts, these unfriendly eyewitnesses could easily have refuted them. But we find no such testimony. We find unbelievers basically attributing Jesus' miracles to demonic deception rather than denying them.

We also have the testimony of the Apostle Paul. He gives a further witness to the ministry of Jesus. The thirteen New Testament letters that were composed by him date from about A.D. 50 to his death in A.D. 64. This is well within the time when unbelieving eyewitnesses could have countered his testimony.

When we consider all the evidence, we conclude the following:

1. Internal evidence from the Gospels leads us to believe they were written a relatively short time after the life of Jesus.
2. Unfriendly eyewitnesses had the opportunity to read and examine what the Gospels testified about Jesus.
3. If the disciples had distorted the facts, we would expect to find Christ's enemies arguing for that. But we do not find this.
4. The Apostle Paul gives further testimony to the life and ministry of Jesus. He also wrote at a time when the eyewitnesses could refute his testimony if it were untrue.
5. Therefore, the New Testament can be considered a reliable record of what Jesus Christ said and did while he was here upon the earth.

9. Has the Text of the New Testament Been Altered as It Has Been Handed Down through History?

Even if the New Testament was originally written at an early date, it would be of no value unless the text of the different books had been transmitted to us reliably. Has the text come down to us in a reliable way or has it been lost or drastically changed?

The New Testament is verified by such an overwhelming amount of evidence that all doubt should be removed as to its reliability. There is no other document in the ancient world that has such abundant evidence to verify its accuracy. Three different lines of evidence are available: (1) Greek manuscripts; (2) translations or versions; (3) writings of the early Christians.

The New Testament was written originally in Greek. Though none of the originals have apparently survived, we do possess an abundance of manuscript copies by which we can reconstruct the text. When we speak of a manuscript copy we refer to handwritten portions that were copied from the original before the invention of printing. There are over 5,500 Greek manuscripts that contain all or part of the New Testament. These date from the early part of the second century up through the fifteenth century. The earliest existing copy, a small fragment from the Gospel of John, can be dated around A.D. 120. There are some fifty other manuscripts or fragments that date within 150 to 200 years from the time of the New Testament's composition.

There are two major manuscripts that date from the first part of the fourth century, Codex Vaticanus A.D. 325, and Codex Sinaiticus A.D. 350. All these manuscripts give abundant testimony to the text of the New Testament.

A further witness can be found in the versions or translations of the New Testament text. Christianity, from its beginnings, has been a missionary religion. At an early date, believers in Christ took his message to other lands. This necessitated translating the New Testament from Greek into other languages. There is an abundance of manuscript testimony (over 18,000) to the New Testament text from the versions. They provide further help in reconstructing the text.

The last line of evidence is the writings of the early Christians. These people wrote, among other things, commentaries on the New Testament and in doing so quoted from the text. Because their testimony is so abundant, the entire New Testament text can be reconstructed from their writings alone. Thus we have a third line of evidence that verifies the New Testament text.

Therefore, three different lines of testimony give sufficient vertification of the New Testament text:

1. Greek manuscripts.
2. Translations from Greek into other languages.
3. Writings of the early Christians.
4. Their witness gives convincing evidence that the New Testament has come down to us intact and that we can trust its testimony.

10. Why Doesn't the Bible Tell Us More of Jesus' Earlier Years?

The New Testament gives the account of the life of Jesus Christ. We are told of the events surrounding his birth and of his ministry to the world. But apart from one incident at age twelve, there is nothing told about his childhood or anything that happened to him until about age thirty.

Thoughout history, fanciful accounts of Jesus' youth have been written but all of these have proven unreliable. The only firsthand source of information we have about the life of Jesus is the New Testament and it remains silent about Jesus' youth. Why the silence? Why doesn't the Scripture give us more details on the childhood and youth of Jesus?

Although the Bible does not give us any specific information on Jesus' early years, we can surmise why it has remained virtually silent on this matter.

The four Gospels basically record the ministry of Jesus to the world. They were not written as biographies but as documents meaning to convey God's truth that Jesus was the Savior sent from heaven. The Gospels record that Jesus did not begin his public ministry until he was about thirty years of age. Whatever happened to him before that time was spent in preparation for this public ministry and is not revealed in Scripture.

But let us not think that these years of silence were unimportant years. Without a doubt Jesus was doing whatever duty that was set before him with the same dedication he would later have in his ministry. His faithfulness is acknowledged at his baptism when God the Father's voice was heard saying, "This is my beloved Son, in whom I am well pleased" (Matt. 3:17). There had been no miracles, no great discourses, nothing as yet done on a grand scale. Yet we know that the Father was pleased with his Son. Whatever things Jesus did during those silent years he did them well, pleasing his heavenly Father, and though we may wish to know more, we can be satisfied with the knowlege that the youth of Jesus was spent as faithful to his calling.

Conclusion to Part I

After investigating the question of the existence of Jesus and the reliability of the records about him, we can conclude the following:

1. *A man named Jesus of Nazareth existed. Both friend and foe testify to that fact.*
2. *The only firsthand information about him is found in the New Testament.*
3. *Those who wrote about Jesus in the New Testament were eyewitnesses to the events that they describe.*
4. *The New Testament was written a short time after Jesus' ascension into heaven.*
5. *The text of the New Testament has an abundance of evidence that assures us the life of Jesus has come down to us accurately.*

We thus conclude that we have to go to the New Testament to get our information about Jesus and that the testimony recorded in the New Testament is accurate.

Now that it has been determined that the New Testament contains a reliable, firsthand account of Jesus' life and ministry, we move on to questions concerning his nature and character, for it is of the utmost importance that we establish the true identity of Jesus.

Who was Jesus?
Was he a man?
Was he God?
Was he Israel's Messiah?
Who did he consider himself to be?

Part II

Jesus: His Nature

*Jesus said, . . . "He who has seen Me
has seen the Father. . . ."*
—John 14:9

Every generation since the time of Jesus has held widely differing opinions concerning Jesus' life, the kind of person he was, and his influence on history.

It is the same today. A recent survey by the Gallup Organization reveals that while the majority of Americans in the 1980s have positive feelings about Jesus, there is much disagreement as to his true nature. Responses to four key questions of the survey show that 70 percent think that Jesus was "not just another man." But only 42 percent believe he was "God among men." Another 27 percent say he was "human but divinely called." And an additional 9 percent feel Jesus was divine because he "embodied the best of humanity."[1]

But in spite of the continuing variety of opinions about the nature of Jesus, there is a constant thread of agreement as to his uniqueness. Secular and Christian writers agree that no man before or after Jesus Christ said or did things like he did. As Gunther Bornkamm writes, "Jesus belongs to this world. Yet in the midst of it he is of unmistakable otherness. This is the secret of his influence and his rejection."[2]

What is the reason for Jesus' uniqueness? In writing about Jesus, Richard C. Halverson, Chaplain of the United States Senate, says, "The fact of Jesus Christ's existence is indisputable. . . . But the minute you accept Him as a fact of history—you cannot explain Him on any other grounds than that He was God in the flesh!

"He was unique in His birth . . .

"He was unique in His life . . .

"He was unique in His death . . .

"He was unique in His victory over death—the Resurrection."[3]

---

1. "How America Sees Jesus," *Eternity,* June 1983.
2. From Gunther Bornkamm, *Jesus of Nazareth,* trans. Irene and Fraser McLuskey, Harper and Row, 1960, p. 56.
3. From *Perspective,* Volume 19, April 12, 1967, Richard C. Halverson.

The Apostle John brings the reason for Jesus' uniqueness into sharp focus when he says, "The Word [God in Jesus Christ] became flesh and dwelt among us" (John 1:14).

How can we best describe the nature of Jesus? There is no better way than to acknowledge he was truly God and truly man . . . the Messiah, our Savior and Redeemer.

11. Was Jesus a Human Being?

Throughout the centuries there have been those who questioned the humanity of Jesus. Some have contended that he was not fully human but only "appeared" to be. The Bible makes it clear that Jesus was fully man.

His birth. Although Jesus was supernaturally conceived, the biblical account of his birth demonstrates that he was a fully human child. "And she brought forth her firstborn Son, and wrapped Him in swaddling cloths, and laid Him in a manger" (Luke 2:7).

When the shepherds saw the newborn babe, they quickly spread the news to others. "Now when they had seen Him, they made widely known the saying which was told them concerning this Child" (Luke 2:17).

When he was eight days old, Jesus was circumcised and brought to the temple for dedication. "And when eight days were completed for the circumcision of the Child, His name was called Jesus, the name given by the angel before He was conceived in the womb. Now when the days of her purification according to the law of Moses were completed, they brought Him to Jerusalem to present Him to the Lord" (Luke 2:21, 22).

In this description of his birth, there is no hint that he was anything other than human. Mary conceived a child; the shepherds spread the word about a child that was born. In the temple he was dedicated in the same manner as any other male child. Although his conception was supernatural, his birth was that of a normal, fully human child.

The remainder of Jesus' life testifies to the fact of his humanity.

His youth. The Scripture states that the child Jesus grew. "And Jesus increased in wisdom and stature, and in favor with God and men" (Luke 2:52). Growing in size and intellectual ability is a human trait. Therefore, this summary statement of his early years testifies to his humanity.

His manhood. After the boy grew to be a man, there is further testimony to his humanity. After his baptism in the Jordan River, Jesus was led by the Spirit out into the wilderness. "And when He had fasted forty days and forty nights, afterward He was hungry" (Matt. 4:2). Here Jesus exhibits the human trait of hunger. Like other human beings, a long period without food made him hungry.

Later in his ministry, the Bible speaks of Jesus being tired from a long trip. "Now Jacob's well was there. Jesus therefore, being wearied from His journey, sat thus by the well" (John 4:6). Jesus was like the rest of humanity in that he became tired.

We are also told that he needed sleep. "And suddenly a great tempest arose on the sea, so that the boat was covered with the waves. But He was asleep" (Matt. 8:24). He had no special ability to stay awake all the time.

Jesus also expressed human emotion. At the tomb of his dead friend, Lazarus, Scripture records, "Jesus wept" (John 11:35). He had human feelings which allowed him to cry at a tragic situation.

A final thing that testifies to his humanity is that he died. "But when they came to Jesus and saw that He was already dead, they did not break His legs" (John 19:33). Like other human beings, Jesus suffered death.

Thus, the Scriptures are united in their testimony to the genuine humanity of Jesus. There is never any indication given that he was somehow nonhuman. He experienced growth, hunger, tiredness, sadness, and death just as other humans experience. He was not given any special immunity from these experiences.

This is important for us to realize. He was born, he lived, and he died, experiencing the same things we do. Therefore, he is able to identify with our feelings when we pray to the Father through him. "For in that He Himself has suffered, being tempted, He is able to aid those who are tempted" (Heb. 2:18). There was no special treatment given Jesus while here on earth. The fact of his humanity was real and is made clear by Scripture.

12. Does the Bible Teach That Jesus Is God?

The Scriptures testify that Jesus was fully human. They also testify that he was God in human flesh. This can be observed from Jesus' own testimony, and the testimony of others.

Jesus' own testimony. From the testimony of Jesus it is clear that he believed himself to be God for he made direct claims to that effect.

He told his disciples on the night of his betrayal, "He who has seen Me has seen the Father" (John 14:9). If one wishes to know what God is like, he need only look at Jesus.

On another occasion, Jesus made himself equal with God the Father: "Therefore the Jews sought all the more to kill Him, because He not only broke the Sabbath, but also said that God was His Father, making Himself equal with God" (John 5:18). The people realized who Jesus was claiming to be and wanted to kill him for it.

Jesus also said, "I and My Father are one" (John 10:30). This again caused the religious leaders to want to stone him. "Jesus answered them, 'Many good works I have shown you from My Father. For which of those works do you stone Me?' The Jews answered Him, saying, 'For a good work we do not stone You, but for blasphemy, and because You, being a Man, make Yourself God' " (John 10:32, 33). Jesus clearly claimed to be God.

The testimony of others. The New Testament gives direct testimony to Jesus being God. "In the beginning was the Word, and the Word was with God, and the Word was God" (John 1:1). This is a clear statement that the Word (Jesus) was in the beginning and he was God.

The Apostle Paul wrote to Titus that believers are "looking for the blessed hope and glorious appearing of our great God and Savior Jesus Christ" (Titus 2:13). Jesus is the "great God" to whom we are looking.

The Apostle Paul told Timothy, "God was manifested in the flesh" (1 Tim. 3:16). This is another direct statement concerning Jesus' identity. Paul testifies that Jesus, as God, became a man.

Thus we have the direct testimony of Jesus and of the writers of the New Testament that he was more than just a man. He was the eternal God who became a man and lived among us.

13. Did Jesus Give Any Indirect Testimony as to His Being God?

We have seen that Jesus made direct claims to be God and that the writers of the New Testament also made direct statements to the same effect. The New Testament also gives indirect evidence that Jesus is God. There are many indirect references that could be cited. Some of these include:

Jesus allowed himself to be worshiped. The God who reveals himself in the Bible has made it clear that he is the only one deserving worship. "You shall have no other gods before Me" (Exod. 20:3).

When Satan wanted Jesus to worship him, Jesus refused saying, "Away with you, Satan! For it is written, 'You shall worship the Lord your God, and Him only shall you serve' " (Matt. 4:10). Jesus testified that worship is something that is reserved for God alone.

Yet, Jesus allowed himself to be worshiped. "And as they went to tell His disciples, behold, Jesus met them, saying, 'Rejoice!' And they came and held Him by the feet and worshiped Him" (Matt. 28:9). "Then he said, 'Lord, I believe!' And he worshiped Him" (John 9:38). If only God is to be worshiped as the Bible testifies, and Jesus allowed himself to be worshiped, then the natural assumption is that Jesus believed himself to be God.

Jesus forgave sins. Another indirect testimony to Jesus' being God is his forgiving sins. In the presence of the religious leaders, Jesus told a sinful woman, "Your sins are forgiven" (Luke 7:48). On another occasion he said to a paralyzed man, "Son, your sins are forgiven you" (Mark 2:5). The religious rulers on both occasions were indignant. They demanded an explanation asking, "Why does this Man speak blasphemies like this?" (Mark 2:7).

No doubt the rulers were remembering God's Word: "I, even I, am He who blots out your transgressions for My own sake" (Isa. 43:25). If only God has the ability to forgive sins and Jesus claimed the ability to forgive sins, then Jesus is claiming to be God.

Jesus claimed he would judge the world. Judgment of the world is something that only God can do. "Then all the trees of the woods will rejoice before the Lord. For He is coming . . . to judge the earth. He shall judge the world with righteousness, and the peoples with His truth" (Psalm 96:12, 13).

Jesus claimed that he would judge the world. "For the Father

judges no one, but has committed all judgment to the Son"
(John 5:22). Only God has the right to judge the world, and
Jesus claimed that he will be that judge. This is more indirect
evidence that Jesus is God.

Therefore, we see that Jesus claimed to be judge of the world
and the forgiver of sin. He also allowed himself to be
worshiped. All of these abilities belong only to God.
Consequently, the indirect evidence testifies that Jesus is God.

14. How Could Christ Be God and Man Simultaneously?

The Bible teaches that Jesus was the eternal God who became
man. How are we to understand his two natures in the one
body? Did each of them work separately? Were they
independent of one another?

When we consider the two natures of Christ, we must be
careful not to divide him into two parts. He was not half-God
and half-man. He was not two persons in one body. He was one
person with two natures. He did not cease being God when he
became a man, neither was he any less man because he was
God. In one body he was God and man united.

Consequently, he did not act as God on some occasions and
then as a man at other times. What Jesus did, he did as the
God-man. Therefore we cannot divide events in his life into the
category of human or divine. He lived and suffered as a human
being, yet all the while he was God.

The two natures of Christ have become permanent. After his
resurrection, Jesus ascended into heaven where he now resides
at the right hand, or place of authority, with God the Father. He
is still the God-man as he will forever be. The Apostle Paul told
Timothy that the man, Christ Jesus, is interceding on our
behalf: "For there is one God and one Mediator between God
and men, the Man Christ Jesus" (1 Tim. 2:5).

The biblical account of Jesus' life demonstrates:

1. Jesus Christ was God and man simultaneously.
2. Though he possessed two natures, they were unified in one
   body. Christ had only one personality, one thought pattern.

3. The life that he lived was lived as the God-man. It is not possible to divide his actions into categories of human or divine.

4. He remains the God-man and forever will be. He suffered this humility because of his great love for us. For all eternity we will be reminded of that as we see him in that body that was sacrificed on our behalf.

15. How Is Jesus Related to God the Father and the Holy Spirit?

The Bible teaches in both the Old and New Testaments that there is one God. The prophet Isaiah records God saying, "Before Me there was no God formed, nor shall there be after Me" (Isa. 43:10). In the New Testament the Apostle Paul told Timothy, "For there is one God" (1 Tim. 2:5). It is the united testimony of Scripture that there is only one God.

But Scripture also testifies that within the nature of the one God there are three distinct personalities. They are named the Father, the Son, and the Holy Spirit. These three personalities are coequal and coeternal. They constitute the one God; this is known as the Trinity. Although the Scriptures do not explain how the one God can be three separate persons, it does clearly teach it.

The Bible teaches that there is a person called the Father, and that person is God. "Paul, an apostle (not from men nor through man, but through Jesus Christ and God the Father)" (Gal. 1:1).

The Scriptures also speak of a second person who is different from the Father. He is called the Son and he, too, is designated God. "In the beginning was the Word, and the Word was with God, and the Word was God" (John 1:1).

There is a third person revealed in Scripture who is different from both the Father and the Son. He is known as the Holy Spirit. He is also called God. "But Peter said, 'Ananias, why has Satan filled your heart to lie to the Holy Spirit . . . ? You have not lied to men but to God' " (Acts 5:3, 4).

Therefore, the Father is God, the Son Jesus is God, and the Holy Spirit is God. Yet as we have seen, the Bible says there is only one God, that the Father, the Son, and the Holy Spirit are the one God. They are one in nature and in purpose, yet distinct in personality. While the Trinity may be beyond our reason and understanding, it is what the Scripture consistently teaches regarding the nature of God.

For example, each member of the Trinity (the Father, the Son, and the Holy Spirit) was involved in Christ's resurrection. Jesus was raised up by the coordinate power of God.

The Bible teaches that God the Father participated in the Resurrection. ". . . just as Christ was raised from the dead by the glory of the Father" (Rom. 6:4).

Jesus was also raised by his own power. "No one takes it from Me, but I lay it down of Myself. I have power to lay it down, and I have power to take it again. This command I have received from My Father" (John 10:18).

The Bible teaches that Jesus was also made alive by the Holy Spirit. "But if the Spirit of Him who raised Jesus from the dead dwells in you, He who raised Christ from the dead will also give life to your mortal bodies through His Spirit who dwells in you" (Rom. 8:11).

Therefore, we have the testimony of Scripture that Christ was raised by the Father, by himself, and by the Holy Spirit.

The mystery of the nature of God as revealed in the Bible includes these teachings:

1. The Bible teaches that one eternal God exists.
2. Within the nature of the one God are three separate persons. They are coequal and coeternal.
3. These three persons are God the Father, God the Son (Jesus) and God the Holy Spirit.
4. Though separate, the three persons of God always work in harmony.
5. The Bible gives examples of the Trinity working together such as at Christ's resurrection.

16. Could Jesus Have Lied about Who He Was?

As we have seen, Jesus made some fantastic claims about who he was. He made himself out to be the eternal God, the Creator of the universe and mankind's only Savior. He consistently made these claims during his time here on earth. The question arises: Is there any evidence that he lied about who he was?

While it is theoretically possible that Jesus lied about who he was, there is certainly no evidence to suggest it. Everything we know about the character of Jesus testifies that he always told the truth.

He underscored the fact that his words were truthful. "The Pharisees therefore said to Him, 'You bear witness of Yourself; Your witness is not true.' Jesus answered and said to them, 'Even if I bear witness of Myself, My witness is true, for I know where I came from and where I am going; but you do not know where I come from and where I am going. . . . I am One who bears witness of Myself, and the Father who sent Me bears witness of Me' " (John 8:13, 14, 18).

If he were a liar, then he was a consistent liar up until the end. He confessed to being the Messiah before his accusers. "And the high priest answered and said to Him, 'I adjure You by the living God that You tell us if You are the Christ, the Son of God.' Jesus said to him, 'It is as you said' " (Matt. 26:63, 64).

This statement caused the Jews to bring him to Pilate to be crucified. "The Jews answered him, 'We have a law, and according to our law He ought to die, because He made Himself the Son of God' " (John 19:7).

The centurion who presided over his crucifixion testified to Jesus' character. "Now when the centurion, who stood opposite Him, saw that He had cried out like this and breathed His last, he said, 'Truly this Man was the Son of God' " (Mark 15:39).

Furthermore, if one contends that Jesus lied about who he was, a motive needs to be found for his lying. People lie to gain the advantage but one becomes hard-pressed to see any advantage in Jesus' lying. What advantage was there to being pressured night and day by the multitudes to perform acts of healing and forgive sin? What advantage was there to being a traveling preacher who had no place to call home? What advantage was there to being put to death for claiming to be the Son of God if he knew his claims were not true? He knew that he could have been released if he had only denied being the Christ.

When we consider that everything we know about Jesus shows he always told the truth and that there was no advantage for him to lie, we see that the suggestion that he lied makes no sense whatsoever. There is no evidence of this and no reason that he would want to do so. As Jesus himself clearly said, "I am the way, *the truth,* and the life" (John 14:6).

17. Could Jesus Have Been Mentally Unbalanced When He Claimed to Be God?

It is clear Jesus made outstanding claims about himself. It is also clear that the evidence leads us to believe that he believed His claims were true. There are some who contend that Jesus made the claims and believed them because he was mentally unbalanced.

There are several problems with this view. From someone deluded or insane, we would expect him to act consistent with his character. That is, someone insane would do and say insane things. When we look at the life and teachings of Jesus we see anything but insanity.

After Jesus delivered the Sermon on the Mount the crowd was awed by his teachings. "And so it was, when Jesus had ended these sayings, that the people were astonished at His teaching, for He taught them as one having authority, and not as the scribes" (Matt. 7:28, 29).

On one occasion the Pharisees sent some of their men to apprehend Jesus. "Then the officers came to the chief priests and Pharisees, who said to them, 'Why have you not brought Him?' The officers answered, 'No man ever spoke like this

Man!' " (John 7:45, 46). The words of Jesus rang clear and true.

Moreover, he handled himself as one always in control every moment. When he was betrayed in the Garden of Gethsemane, he demonstrated self-control and mastery over the situation. " 'Do you think that I cannot now pray to My Father, and He will provide Me with more than twelve legions of angels? How then could the Scriptures be fulfilled, that it must happen thus?' In that hour Jesus said to the multitudes, 'Have you come out, as against a robber, with swords and clubs to take Me? I sat daily with you, teaching in the temple, and you did not seize Me. But all this was done that the Scriptures of the prophets might be fulfilled' " (Matt. 26:53-56).

As we search the Scriptures, we find that there is nothing in the character of Jesus to cause us to believe him to be insane. On the contrary, the depth of his teaching and his masterful character testify that he was indeed the Son of God.

18. Why Did Jesus Say "My Father Is Greater Than I"?

The Bible states that Jesus was God from all eternity. He created the universe and holds it together by his power. This being the case, why did he say to his disciples, "My Father is greater than I" (John 14:28)? How does this statement fit with Jesus being the eternal God?

When one studies the statement in context, the difficulty vanishes. Jesus was talking to his disciples about leaving them and going back to his Father to assume his rightful position. When he is in the presence of his Father, he has no restrictions, no limitations. While he was on earth he took the role of a servant that was in submission to the Father. He had self-imposed limitations, making the Father greater in position than the servant, Jesus. Thus Jesus is not making a statement regarding his nature, for his nature is the same as the Father's. He made that plain earlier: "I and My Father are one" (John 10:30). The reference here is to position. As a servant he took a position of humiliation.

Thus the statement by Jesus does not deny that he is God. It refers to his soon reuniting with the Father and his return to a position without limitations.

19. Why Was Jesus Called the Son of God?

Although those who put their faith in Jesus Christ are called "sons of God," the Scripture designates Jesus as the unique Son of God. What does this title mean?

Jesus referred to himself as the Son of God. "Do you say of Him whom the Father sanctified and sent into the world, 'You are blaspheming,' because I said, 'I am the Son of God'?" (John 10:36).

The demons also recognized Jesus as the Son of God. "And suddenly they cried out, saying, 'What have we to do with You, Jesus, You Son of God?'" (Matt. 8:29).

At his trial, while under oath, Jesus admitted to being the Son of God. "And the high priest answered and said to Him, 'I adjure You by the living God that You tell us if You are the Christ, the Son of God.' Jesus said to him, 'It is as you said'" (Matt. 26:63, 64).

Therefore, it is the united testimony of the New Testament that Jesus was the Son of God. But what does this mean? Are we to take literally the Father-Son relationship that Jesus had with his heavenly Father?

The title "Son of God" does not indicate that Jesus was the literal offspring of his Father. On the contrary, the Bible speaks of Jesus as having existed as God from all eternity. "In the beginning was the Word, and the Word was with God, and the Word was God" (John 1:1). He did not have a beginning as you or I have had.

The title "Son of God" indicates the relationship the Father had to the Son. The Son was equal to the Father, yet he, unlike the Father, became a man. In doing so, he put himself in a position of submission in which he obeyed the will of the Father. The sonship refers to his position as servant, not his nature as being less than God.

We may say therefore that Jesus, through the same substance as the Father, took that relationship of Son upon himself by submitting to the wishes of the Father. As the Son he is no less God, he is merely taking on the role of a servant to show us what God is like and what he requires from us.

20. Why Did Jesus Call Himself the Son of Man?

Jesus' favorite designation, in referring to himself, was the "Son of Man." The Gospels record some seventy-eight times that Jesus used this title for himself. For example, when he asked his disciples about the question of his identity, he said, "Who do men say that I, the Son of Man, am?" (Matt. 16:13).

Though the Bible does not define its exact meaning, the title "Son of Man" probably refers to the fact that Jesus was perfect humanity. He, as God, came down and lived among us as the perfect human being. By doing this, he fulfilled the law of Moses and did what no other human being was able to do. By using this title, he is identifying with the people he had come to save.

The title "Son of Man" was a designation for the Messiah. The Book of Daniel predicted that the Son of Man would inherit God's everlasting kingdom. "And behold, One like the Son of Man, coming with the clouds of heaven! He came to the Ancient of Days, and they brought Him near before Him. Then to Him was given dominion and glory and a kingdom, that all peoples, nations, and languages should serve Him. His dominion is an everlasting dominion, which shall not pass away, and His kingdom the one which shall not be destroyed" (Dan. 7:13, 14).

When Jesus was on trial and was asked if he were the Messiah, he referred to this prediction: "It is as you said. Nevertheless, I say to you, hereafter you will see the Son of Man sitting at the right hand of the Power, and coming on the clouds of heaven" (Matt. 26:64).

This statement infuriated the religious rulers. They accused him of blasphemy for claiming equal authority with God. It was clear to them that Jesus referred to Daniel's prohecy and hence was claiming to be the Messiah.

21. Why Was Jesus Referred to as the Messiah (the Christ)?

One of the major themes of the Old Testament is the coming of the Messiah, or Deliverer. The Hebrew word translated Messiah in its verb form literally means "to anoint." It refers to the process of consecrating the kings and priests to their office by anointing their heads with oil. The noun form of the word is used to refer to kings, "the Lord's anointed" (2 Sam. 19:21).

The term "the Lord's anointed" had a special meaning. It referred to the anointed King who would rule in God's kingdom upon the earth. The Old Testament contains many references to this King and this kingdom, with Messiah (or the Greek form, Christ) being one of the designations for the King.

In Jesus' day, the term Messiah (or Christ) became synonymous with the King who would rule. That is why we find the people asking questions about the Messiah. John the Baptist was asked if he himself were the Christ, to which he replied, "No." The people were divided over the issue of Jesus, whether or not he was the Christ. The New Testament makes it clear that he claimed to be the promised Messiah and that he had the credentials to back up that claim.

Therefore, Jesus is referred to as the Messiah, or the Christ, because that is the special designation of the promised King who would rule in God's kingdom. This title eventually became part of his name. He is now referred to as Jesus Christ. By doing so, we give testimony that Jesus is that special King, the anointed one sent from God.

22. Did Jesus Say He Was the Messiah?

We know that many of the people living in Jesus' day believed him to be the Messiah. We also know that his disciples believed him to be the Promised One. But what about Jesus himself? Did he ever say he was the Messiah or infer that he was the anointed one of God? The answer is a clear yes.

The Scriptures record several instances where Jesus either explicitly or implicitly stated he was the Messiah.

Matthew 11:2-5. In Matthew 11 we find Jesus implying that he is the Promised Messiah. "And when John had heard in prison about the works of Christ, he sent two of his disciples and said to Him, 'Are You the Coming One, or do we look for another?' Jesus answered and said to them, 'Go and tell John the things which you hear and see: The blind receive their sight and the lame walk; the lepers are cleansed and the deaf hear; the dead are raised up and the poor have the gospel preached to them.' "

Jesus answered John by referring to the miraculous deeds he was performing. These were the signs that the Messiah would demonstrate. Isaiah 35:5, 6 lists healing the blind, deaf, and lame as the credentials of the Messiah. Jesus went beyond that promise by healing the lepers and raising the dead. By stating this to the two messengers, he was clearly indicating that he believed himself to be the Messiah and had the credentials to prove it.

Matthew 16:13-17. The disciples of Jesus had seen him perform many mighty works, healing the sick, raising the dead, and preaching the kingdom of God. However, Jesus had never come right out and directly stated he was the Messiah. It was not time for him to reveal clearly his true identity. "When Jesus came into the region of Caesarea Philippi, He asked His disciples, saying, 'Who do men say that I, the Son of Man, am?' So they said, 'Some say John the Baptist, some Elijah, and others Jeremiah or one of the prophets.' He said to them, 'But who do you say that I am?' And Simon Peter answered and said, 'You are the Christ, the Son of the living God.' Jesus answered and said to him, 'Blessed are you, Simon Bar-Jonah, for flesh and blood has not revealed this to you, but My Father who is in heaven.' "

In this instance we see Peter confessing Jesus as the Messiah. Instead of rebuking Peter for error, Jesus agreed with his confession. Jesus then told Peter that it was the heavenly Father who had revealed this truth to him. In this case we have a clear acknowledgment on the part of Jesus that he believed himself to be the Promised Messiah.

Luke 19:37-40. We now come to a third instance where Jesus made it plain that he considered himself to be the Messiah. The setting is Palm Sunday, the triumphal entry of Jesus into Jerusalem.

"Then, as He was now drawing near the descent of the Mount of Olives, the whole multitude of the disciples began to rejoice and praise God with a loud voice for all the mighty works they had seen, saying: 'Blessed is the King who comes in the name of the Lord! Peace in heaven and glory in the highest!' And some of the Pharisees called to Him from the crowd, 'Teacher, rebuke Your disciples.' But He answered and said to them, 'I tell you that if these should keep silent, the stones would immediately cry out.' "

Luke records for us how the people were bestowing upon Jesus the praise that rightfully belonged to the Messiah. When the religious leaders heard what the multitudes were saying, they wanted Jesus to quiet them. Jesus would not do this. He was receiving praise due the Messiah because he was the long-awaited one. Anything less than worship from the multitude would have been wrong. Again we see him acknowledging his true identity.

Matthew 26:63-65. During his trial at the house of Caiaphas, the high priest, Jesus was falsely accused of many things. The trial climaxed with the high priest questioning Jesus concerning his identity. "And the high priest answered and said to Him, 'I adjure You by the living God that You tell us if You are the Christ, the Son of God.' Jesus said to him, 'It is as you said. Nevertheless, I say to you, hereafter you will see the Son of Man sitting at the right hand of the Power, and coming on the clouds of heaven.' Then the high priest tore his clothes, saying, 'He has spoken blasphemy! What further need do we have of witnesses? Look, now you have heard His blasphemy!' "

When Jesus confessed in the affirmative that he was the Christ, the high priest accused him of blasphemy because he claimed to be Israel's Messiah. There were no doubts in the minds of the people present that Jesus believed himself to be the Messiah. Because they did not believe his claim, they wanted to put him to death.

From these accounts there can be no doubt whatsoever that Jesus believed he was the Messiah, the Promised One, who would reveal God's truth to all of mankind.

23. How Is Jesus Different from Any Other Religious Leader?

Throughout history many religious leaders have come on the scene and have attracted large followings. The Buddha, with his teachings on how to cope with life's suffering, gained millions of adherents. Confucius, with his precepts on how members of society should get along with each other, likewise numbers his followers in the millions. The same can be said for Muhammad and the Islamic religion.

This being the case, what makes Jesus so special? Is there anything that separates him from other religious leaders past and present?

Several things make Jesus different. First, Jesus made himself the issue while the other leaders made their teachings the issue. Central to religions such as Buddhism, Islam, Sikhism, Confucianism, etc., are the teachings. What is stressed is what the leaders taught, not so much who they were. The teachers, therefore, are secondary to the teachings.

In Christianity, however, the reverse is true. The all-important issue is not so much what Jesus taught as who he claimed to be. The religious leaders of his day became infuriated when he claimed authority over everything. When Jesus healed on the Sabbath, contrary to their tradition, they became incensed: "Therefore some of the Pharisees said, 'This Man is not from

God, because He does not keep the Sabbath.' Others said, 'How can a man who is a sinner do such signs?' And there was a division among them" (John 9:16). Jesus answered this charge, "For the Son of Man is Lord even of the Sabbath" (Matt. 12:8).

This is one major difference between Jesus and the other religious leaders—he made himself the issue. "He asked His disciples, saying, 'Who do men say that I, the Son of Man, am?' " (Matt. 16:13). He asked this question to secure a commitment either for him or against him. We do not find the leaders of the other world religions doing such a thing.

Another thing that separates Jesus from other religious leaders is that he demonstrated he had authority to make such monumental claims. While other religious leaders have made claims, they gave no legitimate evidence to substantiate them. Jesus, on the other hand, backed up his claims with miracles.

The account of Jesus healing the paralyzed man illustrates this point. When the paralyzed man was brought before him, Jesus said, "Son, your sins are forgiven you" (Mark 2:5). This claim to forgive sins upset the religious rulers. "But some of the scribes were sitting there and reasoning in their hearts, 'Why does this Man speak blasphemies like this? Who can forgive sins but God alone?' " (Mark 2:6, 7).

They were absolutely right in their assertion that only God could forgive sins. Also, making the claim to forgive sins is something that cannot be openly verified. How could anyone have known that Jesus had this authority?

Knowing this to be the case, Jesus responded, " 'Why do you reason about these things in your hearts? Which is easier, to say to the paralytic, "Your sins are forgiven you," or to say, "Arise, take up your bed and walk"? But that you may know that the Son of Man has power on earth to forgive sins'—He said to the paralytic, 'I say to you, arise, take up your bed, and go your way to your house.' And immediately he arose, took up the bed, and went out in the presence of them all" (Mark 2:8-12).

Notice how Jesus dealt with the situation. He asked, "Which is easier to say, your sins are forgiven or rise up and walk?" It is easier to say your sins are forgiven because no one can tell at that moment whether he has been forgiven or not. The forgiveness of sin is not accompanied by some observable sign. But, if someone says, "Rise up and walk," it will immediately become apparent whether or not he has authority. Therefore, Jesus showed the religious rulers he had power in the natural realm over sickness to illustrate that he also had power in the unseen supernatural realm to forgive sin.

Other religious leaders might claim monumental things but they never gave any signs to back up their claims. Jesus not only made the claims, he backed them up with observable miracles that showed he had authority to make them. This point also separates Jesus from other religious leaders.

A final fact that separates Jesus from other religious leaders is that he conquered the ultimate enemy all of us face, death. By coming back from the dead, he provided a concrete answer to the question, What will happen to us when we die? No other religious leader has returned from the dead to verify his claims except Jesus of Nazareth. This fact puts him in a class by himself.

Jesus is different from other religious leaders in at least the following three ways:
1. He made himself the issue rather than his teachings.
2. He backed up his claims with observable miracles.
3. He conquered death to verify that he was the unique Son of God.

24. Was Jesus Involved in Creating the Universe?

Among the many deeds attributed to Jesus is the creation of the universe. The Scripture expressly states that Jesus was involved as Creator. The Gospel of John, in speaking of Jesus, said, "All things were made through Him, and without Him nothing was made that was made" (John 1:3). Here we have the statement that *everything* was created by Jesus. Not one thing has been created apart from him.

The Apostle Paul also testified to Jesus being the Creator. "For by Him all things were created that are in heaven and that are on earth, visible and invisible, whether thrones or dominions or principalities or powers. All things were created through Him and for Him" (Col. 1:16). This comprehensive statement makes it abundantly clear that Jesus created all things in the universe.

Though Jesus was the Creator of all things, this world did not recognize him as such. One of the saddest verses in the Bible testifies to this fact: "He was in the world, and the world was made through Him, and the world did not know Him" (John 1:10). Jesus created the world but when he visited his creation the people did not receive him for who he truly was.

Not only did Jesus create everything in the beginning, he also sustains his creation. The Apostle Paul, after testifying to the creative work of Jesus, wrote, "And He is before all things, and in Him all things hold together" (Col. 1:17, NASB). Jesus is the one who holds the universe together. He is the one who keeps it running in an orderly fashion.

The Book of Hebrews takes this a step further. It teaches that Christ is "upholding all things by the word of His power" (Heb. 1:3). The idea is that Jesus is keeping all things together by his spoken word. Thus, it is the spoken word of Jesus that now upholds the universe.

Jesus Christ created the universe, he sustains it by his spoken word, and he also rules it. The Apostle Paul testified that Christ is "the head over all rule and authority" (Col. 2:10, NASB). The universe and all that is in it is ruled by Jesus.

Presently there is a struggle going on between Jesus and the forces of Satan who are opposing his rule. It is for this reason we have evil in the universe. The Bible, however, teaches that Jesus will someday put an end to those who cause evil. "For He must reign till He has put all enemies under His feet" (1 Cor. 15:25).

Scripture clearly teaches that:

1. Jesus is the Creator of all things.
2. He upholds the universe by his spoken word.

3. He is the rightful ruler of the universe.
4. Satan, who is now opposing Him and who brings evil to the universe, will someday be destroyed along with all things evil.

25. In What Sense Was Jesus a Prophet?

A prophet is a spokesman for God, one who relates the message of God to the people. The Old Testament tells us of many prophets such as Elijah, Jeremiah, and Isaiah. The Old Testament, however, predicted that God would raise up one special Prophet who would be like Moses. Moses wrote, "The Lord your God will raise up for you a Prophet like me from your midst, from your brethren. Him you shall hear" (Deut. 18:15).

But at the time of Moses' death this particular Prophet had not yet appeared. "But since then there has not arisen in Israel a prophet like Moses, whom the Lord knew face to face" (Deut. 34:10). Furthermore, the Old Testament does not record that this particular Prophet *ever* appeared.

At the time of Jesus' coming, the people were still looking for "the Prophet." The religious leaders asked John the Baptist, "Are you the Prophet?" (John 1:21). When Jesus appeared on the scene and started performing his miracles he was recognized by many as the long-awaited Prophet. "Then those men, when they had seen the sign that Jesus did, said, 'This is truly the Prophet who is to come into the world' " (John 6:14).

After the death, resurrection, and ascension of Jesus his disciples made it clear that Jesus was that Prophet like unto Moses. "For Moses truly said to the fathers, 'The Lord your God will raise up for you a Prophet like me from your brethren. Him you shall hear in all things, whatever He says to you. And it shall come to pass that every soul who will not hear that Prophet shall be utterly destroyed from among the people' " (Acts 3:22, 23).

It is therefore the united testimony of Scripture that Jesus was "the Prophet" predicted in the Old Testament who would be like Moses, dealing with God on a face-to-face basis. But Jesus was greater than Moses for he was the only begotten Son who had eternally been face-to-face with the Father. "No one has seen God at any time. The only begotten Son, who is in the bosom of the Father, He has declared Him" (John 1:18).

26. In What Sense Was Jesus a King?

The Old Testament not only looked forward to a Prophet being raised up who was like Moses, it also predicted that Israel would have a king. "When you come to the land which the Lord your God is giving you, and possess it and dwell in it, and say, 'I will set a king over me like all the nations that are around me,' you shall surely set a king over you whom the Lord your God chooses; one from among your brethren you shall set as king over you; you may not set a foreigner over you, who is not your brother" (Deut. 17:14, 15).

This passage goes on to say what the king should and should not do. The type of king called for was never fulfilled by anyone who ruled Israel or Judah. David was the best king that Israel had, and he became the standard of comparison for later kings. But David was far from the ideal king. Scripture records that he was both a murderer and adulterer.

David was given a promise of a king who would be his physical descendant. This man would rule over Israel. "When your days are fulfilled and you rest with your fathers, I will set up your seed after you, who will come from your body, and I will establish his kingdom. He shall build a house for My name, and I will establish the throne of his kingdom forever. . . . And your house and your kingdom shall be established forever before you. Your throne shall be established forever" (2 Sam. 7:12, 13, 16). The immediate fulfillment to this promise was found in David's son, Solomon, who built the first temple in Jerusalem but his kingdom was not eternal. Someone was yet to come and fulfill this prophecy.

The New Testament gives the answer that Jesus Christ was the true King of the Jews. "Then the angel said to her, 'Do not be afraid, Mary, for you have found favor with God. And behold, you will conceive in your womb and bring forth a Son, and shall call His name Jesus. He will be great, and will be called the Son of the Highest; and the Lord God will give Him the throne of His father David. And He will reign over the house of Jacob forever, and of His kingdom there will be no end' " (Luke 1:30-33).

But the objection will be raised that Jesus never ruled as King of the Jews. Quite right. He was the genuine King but was rejected by the unbelieving people. "He came to His own, and His own did not receive Him" (John 1:11). The kingdom, nevertheless, was rightfully his. When Jesus appeared before Pontius Pilate he told the Roman leader the nature of his kingdom. " 'My kingdom is not of this world. If my kingdom were of this world, My servants would fight. . . .' Pilate therefore said to Him, 'Are You a king then?' Jesus answered, 'You say rightly that I am a king. For this cause I was born, and for this cause I have come into the world' " (John 18:36, 37).

The realization of Jesus' kingdom will occur at his second coming. "When the Son of Man comes in His glory, and all the holy angels with Him, then He will sit on the throne of His glory" (Matt. 25:31). Jesus will someday assume his rightful place as King of kings and Lord of lords when he comes again to rule the earth. It is then that the promise made to David, of the everlasting kingdom, will receive its complete fulfillment.

27. Is the Virgin Birth to Be Taken Literally?

The Bible teaches the Virgin Birth, or more properly, the virgin conception of Jesus. The New Testament records the fact that God became a man in Jesus Christ, and the means through which this was accomplished was the Virgin Birth.

The Virgin Birth had been part of the plan of God from the beginning. It was prefigured in the Old Testament. In Genesis 3:15 we read, "And I will put enmity between you and the woman, and between your seed and her Seed; He shall bruise your head, and you shall bruise His heel." The seed of the woman that is referred to here is a prediction of the coming Messiah or Deliverer. He was to be born from the "seed of the woman." This promise gives the first hint of a Virgin Birth.

As the Old Testament history began to unfold it became clear that the Messiah would be virgin born. "Therefore the Lord Himself will give you a sign: Behold, the virgin shall conceive and bear a Son, and shall call His name Immanuel" (Isa. 7:14). There has been considerable controversy about the Hebrew word *almah* used in Isaiah 7:14, whether it means "virgin" or "young woman." Rather than go into a lengthy discussion about this issue we will simply point out the fact that the Old Testament was translated from the original Hebrew into Greek some two hundred years before the time of Christ. When they translated the Hebrew word *almah* in Isaiah 7:14 they used the Greek word *parthenos* which can only mean "virgin." Hence we can observe that before the time of Christ the people understood the passage to refer to a "Virgin Birth."

The New Testament writers make it very clear that Jesus was virgin born. "Now the birth of Jesus Christ was as follows: After His mother Mary was betrothed to Joseph, before they came together, she was found with child of the Holy Spirit. Then Joseph her husband, being a just man, and not wanting to make her a public example, was minded to put her away secretly. But while he thought about these things, behold, an angel of the Lord appeared to him in a dream, saying, 'Joseph, son of David, do not be afraid to take to you Mary your wife, for that which is conceived in her is of the Holy Spirit. And she will bring forth a Son, and you shall call His name Jesus, for He will save His people from their sins.'" (Matthew 1:18-21). Luke 1:26-35 records the same account.

Some have argued that two of the Gospel writers, Mark and John, do not record the Virgin Birth because they knew nothing of it. This argument is unconvincing for the following reasons:
1. Each Gospel writer addresses his work to a particular audience and, in doing so, records a different aspect of the

life of Christ. Mark is emphasizing that Jesus is the servant of the Lord and that he can do the job ordained him to do. Nothing is said in regard to Jesus' birth or early years because it is not relevant to Mark's purpose. The same is true with the Gospel of John. John emphasizes that Jesus was God from all eternity. The Gospel begins in eternity past with Jesus already on the scene. John then stresses the fact that Jesus, as God, became a man, "And the Word became flesh, and dwelt among us" (John 1:14). Consequently he is emphasizing the sublime truth that God came into the world, *not* the manner in which he came.

2. Though Mark and John do not expressly state that Jesus was born of a virgin, nowhere do they teach the contrary. They simply give no details concerning his birth.

3. An argument from silence is usually not a very strong argument. Because someone does not state a fact it does not necessarily follow that that person was unaware of the said fact. It may mean the person, for whatever reason, chose not to mention it.

Also it must be remembered that the Gospel of John implies knowledge of the Virgin Birth without expressly stating it.

Jesus' divine origin had been a cause for argumentation with the religious leaders. He told them that his origin was from heaven. "I speak what I have seen with My Father, and you do what you have seen with your father" (John 8:38). The Jews responded to this by saying that Abraham was their father. Then they made the following accusation at Jesus: "We were not born of fornication" (John 8:41). They accused him of being an illegitimate child. This shows they were aware of the fact that Mary had become pregnant before her marriage to Joseph. This gives further credence to the account of the Virgin Birth as recorded by Matthew, which states that Joseph considered divorcing her privately when he had discovered her pregnancy. In recording this dialogue between Jesus and the religious leaders John implies that the birth of Jesus was not ordinary but came about through unusual circumstances. As Matthew and Luke so clearly tell us, it was not Mary's unfaithfulness that made it an unusual birth, but rather the fact that God had performed a miracle having Jesus conceived not by man but by the Holy Spirit.

Thus we have the testimony of both the Old and New Testament that Jesus of Nazareth, the predicted Messiah, was virgin born.

28. Is It Important to Believe in the Virgin Birth?

We have seen that the Virgin Birth was predicted in the Old Testament in Genesis 3:15 and Isaiah 7:14, and have also observed that the New Testament writers testified to the fact that Jesus was virgin born. But why is this one doctrine so important? Does it matter whether or not Jesus was born of a virgin?

There are at least four reasons why it is important to believe in the Virgin Birth.

The most important reason to hold the belief in the Virgin Birth concerns Jesus' identity as God the Son, the second person of the Trinity. If Joseph were his true father then Jesus would be only a human being. He would not be the Son of God as the Scripture clearly states. He would have had his beginning in time rather than eternally existing. As the Bible states, "In the beginning was the Word, and the Word was with God, and the Word was God" (John 1:1). Thus the Virgin Birth is crucial to Jesus being the Son of God.

A second reason why the Virgin Birth is important concerns the sinless character of Christ. If Jesus had a human father then he would have inherited a sinful nature as the rest of us have. "Therefore, just as through one man sin entered the world, and death through sin, . . . thus death spread to all men, because all sinned" (Rom. 5:12). To the contrary the Scripture states that Jesus never sinned. "Who [Jesus] committed no sin, nor was guile found in His mouth" (1 Pet. 2:22). "And you know that

He manifested to take away our sins, and in Him there is no sin" (1 John 3:5). If Jesus were the son of Joseph, then his sinless character would only be a myth.

A third reason why the Virgin Birth is crucial to the Christian faith concerns our salvation. Without the sinlessness of Christ there would be no salvation. Christ came, according to the Apostle Paul, to save those who were under the law. "But when the fullness of the time had come, God sent forth His Son, born of a woman, born under the law, to redeem those who were under the law, that we might receive the adoption as sons" (Gal. 4:4, 5). This echoes Jesus' own statement, "For the Son of Man has come to seek and to save that which was lost" (Luke 19:10).

God required a sacrifice that was without blemish. "Your lamb shall be without blemish" (Exod. 12:5). If Jesus were a sinner in any sense of the word, then he could not provide salvation for us. However, because he came into the world by supernatural means and lived a sinless life, he could be that sacrifice for our sins without spot and without blemish. The Bible makes this clear: "For He made Him who knew no sin to be sin for us, that we might become the righteousness of God in Him" (2 Cor. 5:21).

The fourth reason to believe in the Virgin Birth is because the Bible says so. If Jesus were not actually born of a virgin then the Bible is wrong. If it is wrong concerning the Virgin Birth, then it is possible that it may be in error about other matters. Once the door opens to the possibility of error in the Scripture the eventual and logical result is that the entire foundation of the Christian faith will crumble. The doctrine of the Virgin Birth and the credibility of Christianity go hand-in-hand.

We conclude that belief in the Virgin Birth is important for the following reasons:
1. The Virgin Birth testifies that Jesus' origin was from heaven and not from earth.

2. If he were the son of Joseph then he would have inherited Joseph's sinful nature.
3. If he were a sinner he could not have offered himself as the perfect sacrifice for our salvation.
4. If Jesus were not Virgin Born then the Bible is in error. We now see that it is necessary that a person believe in the Virgin Birth to have any solid foundation for his faith.

29. How Can a Virgin Birth Be Possible?

Granting that the Scriptures teach the Virgin Birth of Jesus, the question always comes up as to how such an event could be possible. How could this biological feat be accomplished?

It must be stated that the intricate details of how God worked within the body of Mary are not given to us. What is revealed is that the Virgin Birth was a supernatural act of God. "Then Mary said to the angel, 'How can this be, since I do not know a man?' And the angel answered and said to her, 'The Holy Spirit will come upon you, and the power of the Highest will overshadow you; therefore, also, that Holy One who is to be born will be called the Son of God' " (Luke 1:34, 35).

One of the reasons that people deny the Virgin Birth of Jesus is because of its supernatural character. The Scripture, however, makes no excuse for teaching the Virgin Birth. It is a miracle. But it is no more or less miraculous than other events the Bible records. It is inconsistent to accept some of the Bible miracles and yet deny others. If one grants the possibility of God performing miracles, then why, it may be asked, is the Virgin Birth so remarkable? If one can accept at face value the statement of Genesis 1:1, "In the beginning God created the heavens and the earth," it is inconsistent to question his ability to perform any other miracle. If God can speak the universe into existence, he certainly possesses the power to allow a virgin to conceive a child. The God of the Bible has told mankind that he has that power. "Behold, I am the Lord, the God of all flesh. Is there anything too hard for Me?" (Jer. 32:27).

30. Did Jesus Ever Sin?

When we talk about sin we are referring to breaking the law of God. If Jesus had broken the law in any respect then he would be a sinner. The Bible, however, testifies that Jesus never once sinned. This is verified by his own testimony, the testimony of his friends, the testimony of his enemies, and the testimony of God the Father.

Jesus' own testimony. As we examine the account of the life of Jesus, as recorded in the New Testament, we observe that he believed himself to be without sin. When he came to be baptized by John the Baptist, Jesus was momentarily stopped because John realized it was unnecessary. John's baptism was for the confession of sin, and he realized that this one had no sin. But Jesus insisted on being baptized. " 'Permit it to be so now, for thus it is fitting for us to fulfill all righteousness.' Then he allowed Him" (Matt. 3:15). Jesus submitted to the baptism but did not confess any sin.

Immediately after his baptism he was tempted by Satan. Yet Jesus refused to give in to the temptation and told the Devil, "Away with you, Satan! For it is written, 'You shall worship the Lord your God, and Him only you shall serve' " (Matt. 4:10). In the great spiritual battle with the Devil, Jesus did not succumb to sin.

Throughout his ministry Jesus challenged those with him to find sin in his life. "Which of you convicts Me of sin?" (John 8:46). The response from those surrounding him was silence. They had never seen him sin, for he had not sinned.

At the end of his life, while proceeding to the Garden of Gethsemane to be betrayed by Judas Iscariot, Jesus prayed to his heavenly Father saying, "I have glorifed You on the earth. I have finished the work which You have given Me to do" (John 17:4). Knowing of his impending death, his prayer was not one of confession, but rather one of victory. He had finished the mission given to him by the Father and had finished it without committing a sin.

The testimony of his friends. Not only did Jesus recognize that he was sinless, those who knew him were aware of this fact. The Scripture records the attitude of the disciples toward Jesus. They make it clear he was sinless. "Who committed no sin, nor was guile found in His mouth" (1 Pet. 2:22), "And you know that He was manifested to take away our sins, and in Him there is no sin" (1 John 3:5), "For he made Him who knew no sin to be sin for us, that we might become the righteousness of God in Him" (2 Cor. 5:21). The testimony is especially significant because it was given by some of the very same people who lived, ate, and slept with Jesus. They saw him when he was tired, they saw him when he was hungry, they saw him when the multitudes pressed around him. Yet they testified that in all this they never once had seen him sin. Their testimony confirms he was without sin.

The testimony of his enemies. We have heard the testimony of Jesus himself along with the testimony of his friends with regard to his sinlessness. Yet there is another factor to be considered—his enemies. Those who did not believe in him also gave testimony to the fact that he was sinless. As he was casting an evil spirit out of a man this spirit gave testimony to Jesus, saying, "What have we to do with You, Jesus of Nazareth? Did You come to destroy us? I know who You are—the Holy One of God!" (Mark 1:24).

When the traitor Judas Iscariot realized the awful deed which he had done in betraying Jesus he returned to the chief priests and elders, saying, "I have sinned by betraying innocent blood" (Matt. 27:4).

At Jesus' trial those intimately involved in the proceedings admitted they could find no fault in him. "Now the chief priests, the elders, and all the council sought false testimony against Jesus to put Him to death, but found none. Even though many false witnesses came forward, they found none" (Matt. 26:59, 60).

Pontius Pilate, upon examining Jesus, also testified he could find no fault with him. "And when he had said this, he went out again to the Jews, and said to them, 'I find no fault in Him at all' " (John 18:38).

When Jesus died upon the cross the Roman centurion who was watching the proceedings made the following observation: "Certainly this was a righteous Man!" (Luke 23:47).

It is one thing that Jesus' friends recognized his sinlessness; it is quite another thing that his enemies also acknowledged he was without sin.

The testimony of God the Father. The final and by far the most significant testimony that Jesus was sinless came from God the Father.

At Jesus' baptism the Father voiced his pleasure of the Son. "And the Holy Spirit descended in bodily form like a dove upon Him, and a voice came from heaven which said, 'You are My beloved Son; in You I am well pleased' " (Luke 3:22).

Later in his ministry, at the Transfiguration, the Father again voiced audibly that the Son had pleased him. "While he was still speaking, behold a bright cloud overshadowed them; and suddenly a voice came out of the cloud, saying, " 'This is My beloved Son, in whom I am well pleased. Hear Him!' " (Matt. 17:5).

On another occasion, before the multitude, the Father testified to the ministry of the Son. " 'Father, glorify Your name.' Then a voice came from heaven, saying, 'I have both glorified it and will glorify it again' " (John 12:28).

The final act that demonstrated the testimony of God the Father to the sinlessness of Jesus was the acceptance of his sacrifice on the cross. The fact that he received Jesus into heaven showed that his mission was accomplished as the perfect, sinless sacrifice. Jesus' last words were, "Father, 'into Your hands I commend My spirit' " (Luke 23:46). If Jesus had sinned in any manner he would not have been able to appear in the presence of his Father. The Father's unqualified acceptance of Jesus was the final testimony to his sinlessness.

Thus we know that Jesus himself, his friends, his enemies, and God the Father all considered him to be without sin. This being the case we conclude that Jesus lived a perfect, sinless life while here on earth.

31. If Jesus Were without Sin, Why Was He Baptized?

The Bible testifies to the fact that Jesus was without sin. "For we do not have a High Priest who cannot sympathize with our weaknesses, but was in all points tempted as we are, yet without sin" (Heb. 4:15). The Bible also makes it clear that the purpose of baptism is for the public confession of sins. "Then Peter said to them, 'Repent, and let every one of you be baptized in the name of Jesus Christ for the remission of sins' " (Acts 2:38). If only sinners were to be baptized, then why did Jesus submit to it if he were without sin?

This question occurred when Jesus came to John for the purpose of being baptized. John did not want to baptize Jesus because he realized Jesus was the promised Messiah and hence would be without sin. In fact, he tried to prevent it: "And John tried to prevent Him, saying, 'I have need to be baptized by You, and are You coming to me?' " (Matt. 3:14). Jesus' reply is highly instructive: "Permit it to be so now, for thus it is fitting for us to fulfill all righteousness" (Matt. 3:15). After this John baptized Jesus even though he knew him to be sinless.

What then did Jesus mean "to fulfill all righteousness?" The Bible says that Christ came to earth to live the perfect life. This enables him to become the sacrifice for our sins upon Calvary's cross. His life is our example of how we should live. Those who believe in him are instructed to follow that example. Thus he insisted on being baptized to set an example for the conduct of believers.

Furthermore, Jesus, by being baptized, was publicly dedicating himself to do God's will. Even though Jesus had no sin, what better way to begin his ministry than to symbolically identify with sinners.

32. Can Jesus Be Viewed as a Great Prophet or Teacher?

There are those who attempt to sidestep the issue of Jesus' claims. They contend that he was not God, but neither was he lying or deranged. They usually place him in the category of a great teacher, or perhaps the greatest teacher who ever lived. Some go as far as calling him a prophet. But they deny that he was anything more. They deny that he was God.

The possibility that Jesus was only a great teacher does not exist. He very clearly claimed to be more than that. Jesus said to the religious leader, " 'Many good works I have shown you from My Father. For which of those works do you stone Me?' The Jews answered Him, saying, 'For a good work we do not stone You, but for blasphemy, and because You, being a Man, make Yourself God' " (John 10:32, 33).

At the grave of a friend Jesus said, "I am the resurrection and the life. He who believes in Me, though he may die, he shall live. And whoever lives and believes in Me shall never die" (John 11:25, 26). If he were the one whom he claimed to be, then he should be worshiped as God and his teachings diligently followed.

But if Jesus is not all that he claimed to be, then he would either be a liar or insane. A liar or madman would certainly not qualify as a great teacher or prophet, especially if that lie were the central theme of his message. Neither would one want to grant the status of great teacher or prophet to a madman.

The issue is clear. Jesus is either Lord of all or not Lord at all. There is no middle ground, no basis for calling him only a good man, teacher, or prophet.

Conclusion to Part II

The Bible says the following things about the nature of Jesus:
1. *Jesus has been God from all eternity.*
2. *As almighty God he became a human being.*
3. *He was fully human and fully divine. He was not half-God and half-man.*

4. *Jesus is God the Son, the second person of the Trinity.*
5. *He was the long-awaited Messiah of Israel.*
6. *He came into this world by means of a Virgin Birth.*
   Our next section deals with questions concerning his life and ministry here upon the earth.
   Why did Jesus come to earth?
   What was his message?
   Why did he die upon the cross?
   Is there evidence that Jesus rose from the dead?

Part III

Jesus: His Deeds

Now Jesus went about all Galilee,
teaching in their synagogues, preaching the gospel
of the kingdom, and healing all kinds of sickness
and all kinds of disease among the people.
Then His fame went throughout all Syria.
—Matthew 4:23, 24

The Gospel accounts of Jesus' life and ministry, written within the lifetime of contemporaries of Jesus, capture the wonder and drama of Jesus—God himself—moving among the people, demonstrating God's power and love with his amazing deeds.

Jesus made the blind to see. He healed the lepers. He quieted the raging storm. He cast out unclean spirits. He fed five thousand people with five small loaves of bread and two fish. He brought dead Lazarus back to life. And the Gospels record many, many more miraculous acts of Jesus.

We cannot ignore the supernatural aspect of Jesus' deeds. As Bernard Ramm says in his book Protestant Christian Evidences, "The miracles of Jesus . . . involved a great variety of powers. He demonstrated power over nature, as when He turned the water to wine; power over disease, as when He healed the lepers and the blind; power over demons, as was shown by His casting them out; supernatural powers of knowledge, as in His knowing that Nathaniel was under the fig tree; power of creation when He fed 5,000 people from a few loaves and fish; and He exhibited power over death itself in the raising of Lazarus and others."

Jesus explained the reason he performed miracles. It was not to gain political power or wealth. It was to show God's power and to relieve suffering. It was to demonstrate who he was. When the Jewish leaders said to Jesus, " 'If You are the Christ, tell us plainly,' Jesus answered them, 'I told you and you do not believe. The works that I do in My Father's name, they bear witness of me' " (John 10:24, 25).

And at another time, when Jesus was talking with his disciples, he encouraged them: "Believe Me that I am in the Father and the Father in Me, or else believe Me for the sake of the works themselves" (John 14:11).

An old hymn, written before the Civil War, talks about not only the words Jesus taught, but also Jesus' teaching through his deeds. The hymn is also a prayer for Jesus' deeds to touch and teach us today.

Thou didst teach the thronging people
  By blue Galilee;
Speak to us, Thy erring children;
  Teach us purity.

Thou whose touch could heal the leper,
  Make the blind to see;
Touch our hearts and turn from sinning,
  Into purity.

Thou whose word could still the tempest,
  Calm the raging sea,
Hush the storm of human passion,
  Give us purity.

Thou didst sinless meet the tempter.
  Grant, O Christ, that we
May o'ercome the bent to evil,
  By thy purity.
                    —Jemima Luke, 1841

33. Why Did Jesus, as God, Become a Man?

The great truth revealed in the New Testament is that the eternal God became like one of us; he became a human being. "And the Word became flesh and dwelt among us, and we beheld His glory, the glory as of the only begotten of the Father, full of grace and truth" (John 1:14). The Apostle Paul echoes John's thoughts: "Who, being in the form of God, did not consider it robbery to be equal with God, but made Himself of no reputation, taking the form of a servant, and coming in the likeness of men" (Phil. 2:6, 7). In becoming a man Jesus laid aside his heavenly glory to live among us. The question is, why did he do it?

To reveal God to mankind. The Scriptures give us several reasons why Jesus came to earth. The first and foremost reason was to reveal God to mankind. If you wish to know what God is like you need go no further than to look at Jesus. "No one has seen God at any time. The only begotten Son, who is in the bosom of the Father, He has declared Him" (John 1:18). This verse teaches that Jesus explained God to humanity. We need no longer wonder what God is like; Jesus shows us.

To die for the sins of the world. Another reason for Christ's coming was to die on the cross for the sins of the world. "Just as the Son of Man did not come to be served, but to serve, and to give His life a ransom for many" (Matt. 20:28). His death on the cross paid the penalty for our sins. He died in our place so that we do not have to suffer eternally for our misdeeds.

To destroy the works of the devil. His coming also was to destroy the works of the Devil and the hold he has had over mankind. "For this purpose the Son of God was manifested, that He might destroy the works of the devil" (1 John 3:8). Jesus' death on the cross frees us from the power of sin. The Devil no longer has any right to control us because Christ has given us the freedom to choose not to sin.

To be an example for the believer. Jesus also came to provide an example for the believer on how to live one's life. When a person puts his faith in Christ he has an example to follow. Jesus lived the perfect life as the perfect man with faith in his Father. Consequently, we are told "to walk just as He walked" (1 John 2:6).

God became a man to:
1. Show us what he is like.
2. Die on the cross to pay the penalty for sin.
3. Destroy the works of the Devil.
4. Be an example to believers on how we are to live our lives.
   It is for these reasons that Jesus left heaven's glory to live as one of us.

34. Was Jesus' Coming to Earth Predicted?

One of the main things that sets Jesus apart from any religious leader, or anyone else for that matter, is that his coming was predicted. The New Testament gives testimony that Jesus fulfilled the prophecies of the long-awaited Messiah. Jesus himself pointed to the fulfillment of prophecy as testimony to his identity as the Messiah; so did his disciples. Simon Peter wrote, "We also have the prophetic word made more sure, which you do well to heed as a light that shines in a dark place" (2 Pet. 1:19).

The prophecies that Jesus fulfilled were many. Some of them include:

The place of his birth. The Old Testament predicted that the Messiah was to be born in the town of Bethlehem. "But you, Bethlehem Ephrathah, though you are little among the thousands of Judah, yet out of you shall come forth to Me the One to be ruler in Israel, whose goings forth have been from of old, from everlasting" (Mic. 5:2).

The New Testament records this prophecy's fulfillment. "Now after Jesus was born in Bethlehem of Judea in the days of Herod the king, behold, wise men from the East came to Jerusalem, saying, 'Where is He who has been born King of the Jews?' " (Matt. 2:1, 2).

The time of his coming. Another prophecy the Old Testament gave was the time of the coming of the Messiah. "And after the sixty-two weeks Messiah shall be cut off, but not for Himself; and the people of the prince who is to come shall destroy the city and the sanctuary" (Dan. 9:26). This prophecy foretold that the Messiah would come before the city and temple were destroyed.

In A.D. 70 both the city and temple were destroyed by Titus the Roman. Anyone who would make claim to being the Messiah must have appeared on the scene of history before A.D. 70 to literally fulfill Daniel's prophecy. Jesus lived and died some forty years before the destruction of the temple and city.

The Messiah's family tree. The Old Testament gives a specific family line through which the Messiah was to come. He must be a descendant of Abraham (Gen. 12:1-3) through his son Isaac (Gen. 21:12). The Messiah must also be a descendant of Isaac's son Jacob (Num. 24:17). Furthermore, he must come from the tribe of Judah (Gen. 49:10), one of the twelve sons of Jacob. He must be of the family line of Jesse

(Isa. 11:1) and also must be a descendant of Jesse's son David (2 Sam. 7).

The New Testament begins by showing that Jesus was from the proper family line. "The book of the genealogy of Jesus Christ, the Son of David, the Son of Abraham" (Matt. 1:1).

All of the above requirements were met by Jesus at his birth. He was born in the proper city, at the right time in history, through the correct family line. Each of these prophecies was beyond Jesus' ability for deliberate fulfillment. He had no control over where, when, or to whom he was to be born. Yet at his birth he fulfilled these predictions. He went on to fulfill many other prophecies of the Messiah. These few are given to show that his coming to earth was not only different than any religious leader before or since, his coming was also supernatural.

35. Why Did Jesus Come to Earth at That Particular Time in History?

The question often comes up as to why Jesus came to earth at the specific time that he did. Why didn't he come at another time which perhaps could have been better suited to spread his message? In the secular rock musical, *Jesus Christ Superstar*, this question was asked by Judas in his song:

Every time I look at you I can't understand
Why you let the things you do get so out of hand.
It would have turned out better if you had it planned.
Why did you pick such a backward time in such a strange
*   land?*
If you'd come today you would have reached the whole
*   nation.*
Israel in 4 B.C. had no mass communication.

Could Jesus have picked a better time to arrive in history? Was there any special reason he came when he did?

The Bible is clear that Jesus came at the prescribed time. "But when the fullness of the time had come, God sent forth His Son, born of a woman, born under the law, to redeem those who were under the law" (Gal. 4:4, 5).

His coming had been predicted in the Old Testament. Jesus upbraided the people for not knowing the time of his coming. "If you had known, even you, especially in this your day, the things that make for your peace! But now they are hidden from your eyes. For the days will come upon you when your enemies will . . . surround you and close you in on every side . . . and they will not leave in you one stone upon another, because you did not know the time of your visitation" (Luke 19:42-44). All the signs had been given, the prophecies fulfilled regarding his coming, yet the people still rejected him.

Though everything indicates that Jesus came according to God's schedule, nothing is said in Scripture about why he chose that time in history.

Reasons have been given to demonstrate his coming was at an opportune time. There was a universal language—Greek. There was peace in the Roman Empire which aided the spread of his message, and there was an excellent road system throughout the Roman Empire which allowed for easy travel. Yet none of these facts explains why he came when he did. God is silent on that matter except to say it was at the perfect time. To assume things would be different if instead he had chosen to come in the twentieth century is untrue. Twentieth-century man has sufficient reason to believe in Jesus. The fact that he chose to come some two thousand years ago does not change the fact that he came and fulfilled that which the Bible had predicted.

36. What Did Jesus Look Like?

A question that is asked frequently concerns the physical appearance of Jesus. People wonder if Scripture gives any direct testimony as to what Jesus looked like physically. The answer is no. There is nothing in the Bible that describes the physical characteristics of Jesus. There are, however, a few indirect references that give us some idea of what he looked like.

We can surmise from the Scripture that Jesus was not outstanding in his appearance. He was probably of average size for a man living in his day. We can deduce this from the record of his betrayal. Judas Iscariot made a pact to betray Jesus for thirty pieces of silver. The chief priests and religious rulers wanted to be sure they had the right man. Judas said, "Whomever I kiss, He is the One; seize Him" (Matt. 26:48). If Jesus had been above average in height or had some outstanding physical characteristic, then it is hard to imagine why Judas needed to point him out. Jesus obviously did not stand out that strikingly in a group of eleven other men.

At his resurrection, Mary Magdalene first thought Jesus was the gardener. Again, if he had some unmistakable physical characteristic, then it would be difficult to imagine him being taken for a gardener. Even though Mary was not expecting a resurrected Christ, any outstanding physical characteristic would probably have been noticed.

Some take the prophecy that Isaiah makes of the Messiah to indicate that he was ugly or deformed. "He has no form or comeliness; and when we see Him, there is no beauty that we should desire Him" (Isa. 53:2). But this prophecy more likely refers either to the battered condition of his body while on the cross, or that he was just average in his looks. Moreover, it does not explain why Jesus had to be singled out of a crowd. If he were somehow deformed, there would have been no need for a sign from Judas. Also the Scripture tells us that little children came to Jesus of their own accord. Usually children are afraid of a physical deformity because of a natural fear of the unknown. This would further indicate that there was nothing unusual about Jesus' appearance.

In the Old Testament, the sacrificial lamb was to be without spot or blemish. This was a picture of Jesus, the Lamb of God, who was the perfect sacrifice for our sin. Although the perfection of Jesus was spiritual, that is, he was without sin, it might also have reference to his physical characteristics. But of this point we cannot be sure.

Thus anything we can deduce about Jesus' physical appearance is only from inference. This indicates that his outward appearance was not that crucial. What was important was what was on the inside—in his heart. Many years before Jesus came, God had made that clear. "For the Lord does not see as man sees; for man looks at the outward appearance, but the Lord looks at the heart" (1 Sam. 16:7).

37. Did Jesus Have Brothers and Sisters?

The birth of Jesus was the result of a supernatural union between God and Mary. She was a virgin at the time when Jesus was conceived. There are some who maintain that Mary remained a virgin throughout her life. If this was the case, then Jesus would have been an only child. The Scriptures, however, indicate that Jesus did have brothers and sisters.

The first testimony that Mary did not remain a virgin can be found in the first chapter of Matthew. When Joseph had discovered that Mary was going to have a child he decided to secretly divorce her. He had not had sexual relations with her and knew the child was not his. But an angel appeared to Joseph in a dream and told him that his wife's pregnancy was through God, the Holy Spirit. Matthew tells us: "Then Joseph, being aroused from sleep, did as the angel of the Lord commanded him and took to him his wife, and did not know her till she had brought forth her firstborn Son. And he called His name Jesus" (Matt. 1:24, 25). From this Scripture we can determine that Joseph did not have sexual relations with Mary until after the birth of Jesus. Thus this passage refutes any idea of the perpetual virginity of Mary.

Furthermore, Scripture gives testimony to the fact that Joseph and Mary had other children who were the brothers and sisters of Jesus. "While He was still talking to the multitudes, . . . one said to Him, 'Look, Your mother and Your brothers are standing outside, seeking to speak with You.' But He answered and said to the one who told Him, 'Who is My mother and who are My brothers?' And He stretched out His hand toward His disciples and said, 'Here are My mother and My brothers! For whoever does the will of My Father in heaven is My brother and sister and mother' " (Matt. 12:46-50).

On another occasion we are told the people in his hometown of Nazareth became indignant at his claims. " 'Is this not the carpenter, the Son of Mary, and brother of James, Joses, Judas, and Simon? And are not His sisters here with us?' And they were offended at Him" (Mark 6:3).

Who were these brothers and sisters of Jesus? There are two scriptural possibilities. There were either children born to Mary and Joseph after Jesus, hence his younger brothers and sisters, or children of Joseph from a previous marriage.

The reason some believe that these were not children of Joseph and Mary is due to the way they are designated. In Mark 6:3 Jesus is called the "Son of Mary" and is distinguished separately from the brothers who are named as well as his sisters.

In Acts 1:14 we read that included in the group in the upper room were "Mary the mother of Jesus, and . . . His brothers." Here they are called his brothers not her sons. This has led some to speculate that they were sons of Joseph from a previous marriage. Others have contended that they were first cousins of Jesus, the sons of Cleopas who was supposedly a brother or brother-in-law of Joseph. But this view has no scriptural support.

Although one cannot be absolutely sure on the matter, the natural sense in which to take it is that they were his younger brothers and sisters. We are told by John that during the ministry of Jesus "even His brothers did not believe in Him" (John 7:5). This would seem to indicate full brothers rather than half-brothers, but again one cannot be absolutely sure. What we can be sure of, however, is that Scripture does not rule out the possibility of Jesus having brothers and sisters born to Joseph and Mary.

38. What Does It Mean, Jesus "Emptied Himself" When He Came to Earth?

The Apostle Paul, in writing to the church at Philippi, taught that Christ "emptied himself" while here upon the earth. "Have this attitude in yourselves which was also in Christ Jesus, who, although He existed in the form of God, did not regard equality with God a thing to be grasped, but emptied Himself, taking the form of a bond-servant, and being made in the likeness of men. And being found in appearance as a man, He humbled Himself by becoming obedient to the point of death" (Phil. 2:5-8, NASB).

Many questions have surrounded this matter of Jesus emptying himself. What exactly did he empty himself of? His divine attributes? What was this emptying all about?

First, it must be stated that the Scriptures do not teach that Christ set aside certain of his divine attributes (such as being all-knowing, all-powerful, and everywhere-present) when he came to earth. If Jesus was God, as the Scripture teaches, it is hard to imagine how he could somehow rid himself of these qualities and still be God. The emptying could not have been with regard to his attributes as God, because, by definition, God cannot cease being God.

What the passage before us in Philippians teaches is not the emptying of Jesus' divine attributes when he was on earth, but rather the independent use or exercise of these attributes apart from the will of the Father. Philippians 2:6 tells us that equality with God was not something Jesus had to grasp, for he was, by nature, God. Philippians 2:7, 8 gives us the solution. Christ came as a servant who humbly obeyed the Father. He was God yet he was also a man. In his earthly state he submitted himself to the will of the Father. The glory which he previously had as the only begotten Son was temporarily laid aside when he came to earth. At the end of his life he prayed to his Father to restore his former glory. "I have glorified You on the earth. I have finished the work which You have given Me to do. And now, O Father, glorify Me together with Yourself, with the glory which I had with You before the world was" (John 17:4, 5).

Jesus chose not to independently exercise his divine powers while here upon the earth. Jesus chose rather to live the life as a servant who put his trust in his heavenly Father. The following statements from Jesus illustrate this truth: "I do not seek My own will but the will of the Father who sent Me" (John 5:30); "For I have come down from heaven, not to do My own will, but the will of Him who sent Me" (John 6:38).

Jesus chose to submit to the will of God the Father in every word and in every deed. Therefore, any independent desire on Jesus' part to act apart from God the Father was emptied or laid aside while here upon the earth.

39. Didn't Jesus Come to Bring Peace on Earth?

When the angel announced the birth of Jesus, the host of heaven appeared with him and praised God in these familiar words saying, "Glory to God in the highest, and on earth peace, good will toward men" (Luke 2:14). The question then arises: Didn't Jesus come to earth to bring peace? If so, then he failed in his mission because the world has not known peace since his coming. Yet the idea of Jesus coming to earth for the purpose of bringing a lasting peace is contrary to his words.

Although one of the designations of Jesus is the "Prince of Peace," his first coming was not for the purpose of bringing peace on earth. He made this clear, "Do not think that I came to bring peace on earth. I did not come to bring peace but a sword. For I have come to 'set a man against his father, a daughter against her mother, and a daughter-in-law against her mother-in-law.' And 'a man's foes will be those of his own household' " (Matt. 10:34-36).

According to his own words Jesus came to testify of the truth. He told Pilate that he came into the world to "bear witness to the truth. Everyone who is of the truth hears My voice" (John 18:37).

The nature of Jesus' message called for people to make a choice. Rather than uniting humanity, it divided friends and families. It still has that effect today. Those who believe in Jesus are separated from those who do not believe. His mission was not that of bringing peace but rather bringing the truth of God.

One day he will return and then establish an everlasting kingdom where peace will be the rule rather than the exception. Until that time the message of Jesus divides those who love God's truth from those who do not.

40. Why Was Jesus Tempted by the Devil?

The baptism of Jesus was his inauguration into the public ministry. He received the confirmation of his identity from God the Father and God the Holy Spirit. The Father's voice was heard identifying the Son, and the Holy Spirit came upon him in the form of a dove. "And the Holy Spirit descended in bodily form like a dove upon Him, and a voice came from heaven which said, 'You are my beloved Son; in You I am well pleased' " (Luke 3:22). Now that Jesus had been commissioned and confirmed he was about to receive his first test. The test would come from the Devil.

"Then Jesus was led by the Spirit into the wilderness to be tempted by the devil" (Matt. 4:1). After fasting forty days he was hungry. Because Jesus was fully human he, like the rest of us, had the need for food. It was at this time that the Devil perceived him to be the most vulnerable. The Gospels record three of the temptations that Jesus went through. The temptations were Satan's attempt to get Jesus to act independently of the will of the Father, and to exploit his Messiahship to his own advantage.

Stones into bread. The first temptation of Satan to a hungry Jesus was to turn stones into bread.

"Now when the temptor came to Him, he said, 'If You are

85

the Son of God, command that these stones become bread.' But he answered and said, 'It is written, "Man shall not live by bread alone, but by every word that proceeds from the mouth of God" ' " (Matt. 4:3, 4).

There is nothing inherently wrong about turning stones into bread but in this case Jesus had no command from the Father to cease the fast. The Devil was attempting to get Jesus to act independently of the Father to satisfy an immediate desire. Jesus refused and won the first round.

Jump from the temple. The Devil would not give up easily. Matthew records a second temptation.

"Then the devil took Him up into the holy city, set Him on the pinnacle of the temple, and said to Him, 'If You are the Son of God, throw Yourself down. For it is written: "He shall give His angels charge concerning you," and, "In their hands they shall bear you up, lest you dash your foot against a stone." ' Jesus said to him, 'It is written again, "You shall not tempt the Lord your God" ' " (Matt. 4:5-7).

This temptation would have Jesus putting God to a needless test. It would have put Jesus on the same level of other religious figures who perform a supernatural sideshow to get the people's attention. Miracles would be a part of Jesus' ministry but they would always be done with a clear purpose. Jumping from the temple would detract from the restrained and dignified character of God.

Worship Satan. A third temptation was Satan offering Jesus the kingdoms of the world if he would worship him.

"Again, the devil took Him up on an exceedingly high mountain, and showed Him all the kingdoms of the world and their glory. And He said to Him, 'All these things I will give You if You will fall down and worship me.' Then Jesus said to him, 'Away with you, Satan! For it is written, "You shall worship the Lord your God, and Him only you shall serve" ' " (Matt. 4:8-10).

If Jesus were to receive the lordship of all the world's kingdoms it would come from God the Father, not from the Devil. This temptation of Satan had another subtle appeal; if Jesus would bow to him, he would not have to receive the kingdoms by way of the cross at Calvary. No pain, no suffering, if he would bow down. Although the way of the cross was not the easiest way, it certainly was the purpose of Jesus coming into the world. "Just as the Son of Man did not come to be served, but to serve, and to give His life a ransom for many" (Matt. 20:28).

On another occasion Simon Peter rebuked Jesus for predicting his death on the cross. To this Jesus gave a swift reply: "Get behind Me, Satan! You are an offense to Me, for you are not mindful of the things of God, but the things of men" (Matt. 16:23). This clearly reveals that the cross was God's way. Any other way for Jesus to go was not appropriate.

The temptation of Jesus and his response to Satan revealed several important truths:

1. Jesus was dedicated to completing the mission given him in the manner that the Father prescribed. He knew what he had come to do and he was going to do it. On a later occasion he would tell the religious rulers, "Even if I bear witness of Myself, My witness is true, for I know where I came from and where I am going; but you do not know where I came from and where I am going" (John 8:14).

2. Satan was unsuccessful in deterring Jesus from his mission. Although Satan would try again, his doom was sealed. Shortly before Jesus' death, Satan again tried to get him to turn from God's way but Jesus would not give in. He said to his disciples, "I will no longer talk much with you, for the ruler of this world is coming, and he has nothing in Me" (John 14:30).

3. The believer should be encouraged. Jesus went through suffering and testing, as all of us do, yet without sinning. As a result, he understands the temptations we face having

gone through them himself. "For in that He Himself has suffered, being tempted, He is able to aid those who are tempted" (Heb. 2:18).

4. Last, and most important, because Jesus resisted the temptation of the Devil, he demonstrated that he would be the perfect sacrifice. Jesus had come to earth to die for the sins of the world but his death would be effective only if he were without sin. The victory here over Satan set the stage for him being that sacrifice. The Scripture later testifies, "Knowing that you were not redeemed with corruptible things, like silver or gold, from your aimless conduct received by tradition from your Fathers, but with the precious blood of Christ, as of a lamb without blemish and without spot" (1 Pet. 1:18, 19).

Jesus was victorious over each temptation. He resisted each of Satan's offers. In doing so, he demonstrated the truth that he was upon the earth not to do his own will but the will of the Father.

41. Why Did John the Baptist Ask Jesus If He Were the Messiah?

There is a question that the Gospels raise concerning John the Baptist and his view of Jesus. John the Baptist, the forerunner of Christ, pointed Jesus out as the Messiah. "The next day John saw Jesus coming toward him, and said, 'Behold! The Lamb of God who takes away the sin of the world!' " (John 1:29).

John clearly identified Jesus as the Messiah. Yet we have the later account of John being put in prison by King Herod. The Baptist then sent two messengers to Jesus asking him if he were the Christ or if they should look for another. Jesus answered in such a way that left no doubt that he was the Messiah. "Go and tell John the things you have seen and heard: that the blind see, the lame walk, the lepers are cleansed, the deaf hear, the dead are raised, the poor have the gospel preached to them" (Luke 7:22). John certainly would have understood this message, for the signs Jesus was performing were the credentials of the Messiah.

But why did John originally ask the question? Had he been mistaken about Jesus? Had Jesus let him down? Had John wavered in faith? There is a better answer than assuming John had doubts about Jesus' identity or that he was in some sort of depression while in prison.

The answer would seem to lie in the circumstances of the nation Israel. Jesus came into the world when Rome ruled the Jewish people with an iron hand. There were many in Palestine who were proclaiming that the coming kindgom, predicted in the Old Testament, would come by means of a military overthrow. But Jesus came on the scene and proclaimed God's kingdom was at hand but said it would belong to the meek, not the strong. His ministry was one of mercy, not judgment. "For God did not send His Son into the world to condemn the world, but that the world through Him might be saved" (John 3:17). This message of Jesus' was revolutionary. He told the people to go the extra mile, to turn the other cheek, to submit rather than resist.

John the Baptist, on the other hand, proclaimed the vengeance the Messiah would bring on the unbelievers: "Brood of vipers! Who has warned you to flee from the wrath to come? Therefore bear fruits worthy of repentance, and do not think to say to yourselves, 'We have Abraham as our father.' For I say to you that God is able to raise up children to Abraham from these stones. And now even the ax is laid to the root of the trees. Therefore every tree which does not bear good fruit is cut down and thrown into the fire" (Matt. 3:7-10). John was probably wondering how the kingdom could be established in the manner Jesus prescribed. His question contains the idea that Jesus was not going about it fast enough. Jesus' answer indicates that the program was underway, but according to his schedule and not John's. The day of vengeance is something still awaiting the unbelievers in the future.

It seems best to take John's question as one concerned more with the tactics of Jesus in establishing his kingdom, rather than John questioning Jesus' identity as Messiah.

42. If Jesus Had the Credentials of the Messiah, Why Didn't the Jews Accept Him?

A question that often is raised concerns the credentials of Jesus and the unbelief of the nation Israel. If Jesus did possess the proper credentials of the promised Messiah and presented them to the nation, as the New Testament records, then why didn't the people believe in him? What was it that caused the majority of people to reject him?

Though there were many factors that led to the Jewish people rejecting Jesus as their Messiah, it can be stated simply: they did not believe because they did not want to believe. It is the same reason why most people throughout history have rejected Jesus as Messiah. It is not that they could not believe, it is that they would not believe. It is not that people need more evidence, it is that they do not act upon the evidence that they have.

The religious leaders at the time of Jesus were corrupt. Their leadership was indicative of the spiritual state of the people. Though the people went through the proper rituals that God had commanded, their hearts were not in them. They were not that interested in the truth of God.

The New Testament provides many such examples of the religious leaders attempting to suppress the truth of God. A case in point is that of Lazarus. In the presence of the religious rulers, Jesus brought back Lazarus from the dead after Lazarus had been dead four days. One would think that such a miracle would at least make them consider believing in Jesus as the Messiah, because from their own testimony they never saw anyone do such miracles. But discussing about what to do with Jesus, they decided to kill him. "Then from that day on they plotted to put Him to death" (John 11:53). Rather than causing belief, it made them want to get rid of him. But it was not only Jesus that they wanted to kill.

Lazarus was walking around alive, a living testimony to the power and credentials of Jesus. Therefore, the religious leaders wanted to kill Lazarus also! "But the chief priests took counsel that they might also put Lazarus to death, because on account of him many of the Jews went way and believed in Jesus" (John 12:10, 11).

Jesus, in speaking to his disciples, summed up the state of the people: "Seeing they do not see, and hearing they do not hear, nor do they understand" (Matt. 13:13). The basic reason that the majority of the nation Israel rejected Jesus is simply because they did not want to believe.

43. Was Jesus Always Confident of His Identity?

The Bible testifies that Jesus is the eternal God who became a man in order to sacrifice his life for the sins of the world. This brings up certain questions. Was this something he was always aware of? Was there ever a time Jesus doubted his calling? Or, could it be possible that he was overwhelmed by all the attention he received and allowed himself to be taken for someone he was not?

The Bible is clear that Jesus was always confident of who he was and why he had come to earth. From our first glimpse of him, until the end of his life, we find Jesus confident in his person and message.

The first encounter we have of him, apart from the birth record, is at age twelve. "His parents went to Jerusalem every year at the Feast of the Passover. And when He was twelve years old, they went up to Jerusalem according to the custom of the feast. When they had finished the days, as they returned, the Boy Jesus lingered behind in Jerusalem. And Joseph and His mother did not know it; but supposing Him to have been in the company, they went a day's journey, and sought Him among their relatives and acquaintances. So when they did not find

Him, they returned to Jerusalem, seeking Him. Now so it was that after three days they found Him in the temple, sitting in the midst of the teachers, both listening to them and asking them questions. And all who heard Him were astonished at His understanding and answers. So when they saw Him, they were amazed; and His mother said to Him, 'Son, why have You done this to us? Look, Your Father and I have sought You anxiously.' And He said to them, 'Why is it that you sought Me? Did you not know that I must be about My Father's business?' " (Luke 2:41-49).

From this account we see that at the age of twelve Jesus knew who he was and that he had a mission from God the Father.

During his public ministry, his confidence in his calling was sure. He told the religious rulers, "You are from beneath; I am from above. You are of this world; I am not of this world" (John 8:23).

If there ever was a time when one would expect Jesus to have doubts who he was, it would have been during his betrayal and death. But in the face of this great adversity, he never denied who he was or the calling that he had.

In the Garden of Gethsemane, "He was withdrawn from them about a stone's throw, and He knelt down and prayed, saying, 'Father, if it is Your will, remove this cup from Me; nevertheless not My will, but Yours, be done' " (Luke 22:41, 42). Jesus knew what he was about to face and he faced it without wavering.

At his trial, Jesus confessed to being the Christ: "And the high priest answered and said to Him, 'I adjure You by the living God that You tell us if You are the Christ, the Son of God.' Jesus said to him, 'It is as you said' " (Matt. 26:63, 64). He realized that this confession would lead to his eventual death. If he had any doubts about his calling, the trial was his chance to set the record straight. Yet he made it clear that he believed himself to be the Christ.

Thus the Bible testifies that from the age of twelve until his death on the cross there was no hesitancy on Jesus' part concerning who he was or why he had come to earth.

44. Could the Teachings of Jesus Have Come from a Different Source Than God?

Throughout the history of the Christian church there have been those who have tried to explain Jesus' teachings by attributing them to influences he or the early Christians received. These include: (1) Jesus went to India or Egypt and derived his teachings from religious masters in those countries; (2) Jesus' teachings came from the Essene community, a group of ascetic Jews living on the edge of the Dead Sea who copied ancient manuscripts onto the Dead Sea Scrolls; (3) Jesus based his teachings on the various "mystery religions" that were popular in the Roman Empire.

These three theories are representative of what has been taught down through the centuries. Though the theories are different, they all have one thing in common: they deny Jesus' teachings were from God the Father. If this is true, then Jesus was not the Son of God as the New Testament testifies.

These theories lack convincing evidence to support their contention that Jesus "borrowed" his teaching. The differences between Jesus' teaching and these supposed sources are much greater than any similarity.

But there is a greater problem in proposing any of these theories. Jesus not only said his teachings were from God, he demonstrated that he had the authority to make the claims that he did. His miracles have been verified by eyewitness testimony. If he were only another religious leader then how was he able to perform the miracles which he did, including that of the Resurrection?

The issue is clear when it comes to determining the source of Jesus' teaching. An answer needs to be found by taking into consideration his miraculous life. Simplistic parallels that are drawn from other religions at the time do not in any way explain his teachings or how he was able to perform miracles.

Jesus made it clear where his doctrine came from. "My doctrine is not Mine, but His who sent Me. If anyone wants to do His will, he shall know concerning the doctrine, whether it is from God or whether I speak on My own authority" (John 7:16, 17).

45. Why Did Jesus Disrupt the Temple?

Many people think of Jesus as someone meek and mild who would never raise his voice or be upset at anything. Consequently, they have a hard time understanding the Gospel accounts of him going into the temple and disrupting the activities of the moneychangers. Why did he do it and why was he so upset?

John records what occurred: "Now the Passover of the Jews was at hand, and Jesus went up to Jerusalem. And He found in the temple those who sold oxen and sheep and doves, and the moneychangers doing business. When He had made a whip of cords, He drove them all out of the temple, with the sheep and the oxen, and poured out the changers' money and overturned the tables. And He said to those who sold doves, 'Take these things away! Do not make My Father's house a house of merchandise!' " (John 2:13-16).

Is this an example of Jesus losing his self-control? Hardly. Instead, his response to the moneychangers shows how seriously Christ felt about and dealt with corruption. His actions demonstrated that he would accomplish the task, which God the Father had sent him to do, in an uncompromising manner.

This was the first Passover (a seven-day feast commemorating the nation Israel's deliverance from the bondage of Egypt) that Jesus celebrated after beginning his public ministry. When Jesus arrived at the temple he found it in a state of abuse. At the entrance of the temple there were moneychangers, who were charging exorbitant rates, and droves of people buying and selling the animals prescribed for sacrifice.

This first act of his public ministry in the city of Jerusalem made it clear that he detested the religious practices that were going on. There was no sermon, no gentle chiding of the people. Extreme abuse called for extreme measures. With a godly zeal he took a cord and swung it at the moneychangers and the men who were selling the animals and drove them all, animals included, out of the temple area. He ordered them to stop making God's house of prayer into a place of thievery.

There is no apology for what Jesus did. The corruption of the temple area testified to the sad spiritual state that the nation was in. Jesus' reaction was clear and decisive. The temple area needed to be cleansed because of the corruption going on there. The public ministry of Jesus began by him doing just that. The Bible also records a second disruption of temple business by Jesus at the end of his ministry. Those who corrupted the temple did not learn their lesson the first time. The truth of God was rejected in the place which should have welcomed it the most.

46. What Significance Did the Transfiguration Have?

The Transfiguration was the glorification of the human body of Jesus. On this occasion his body underwent a change in form, a metamorphosis, so that it shone as brightly as the sun. At the time of the Transfiguration, Jesus' earthly ministry was coming to a close. He had acknowledged that he was the Messiah and predicted his death and resurrection. Now he was to reveal, to a select few, his divine glory.

The Bible gives this account: "Jesus took Peter, James, and John his brother, brought them up on a high mountain by themselves, and was transfigured before them. His face shone like the sun, and His clothes became as white as the light. And behold, Moses and Elijah appeared to them, talking with Him. . . . A bright cloud overshadowed them; and suddenly a voice came out of the cloud, saying, 'This is My beloved Son, in whom I am well pleased. Hear Him!' And when the disciples heard it, they fell on their faces and were greatly afraid. But Jesus came and touched them and said, 'Arise, and do not be afraid.' And when they had lifted up their eyes, they saw no one but Jesus only" (Matt. 17:1-3, 5-8).

Jesus told Peter, James and John not to tell anyone about this until after he had risen from the dead. Some years later Simon Peter would write of this event: "For we did not follow cunningly devised fables when we made known to you the power and coming of our Lord Jesus Christ, but were eyewitnesses of His majesty. For He received from God the Father honor and glory when such a voice came to him from the Excellent Glory: 'This is My beloved Son, in whom I am well pleased.' And we heard this voice which came from heaven when we were with Him on the holy mountain" (2 Pet. 1:16-18).

The Transfiguration provides further evidence that Jesus was the divine Son of God. It is not coincidental that this happened soon after Jesus had acknowledged himself to be the Christ, the one who left heaven's glory to come to earth. Now three of his disciples were to get a glimpse of that glory.

The appearance of Moses and Elijah with Jesus is highly significant. The name Moses was equated with the Old Testament law that God had given to the people. Jesus came and fulfilled the commandments of the law and did the things the law could not do, that is, to provide an answer for the problem of sin. The law pointed out the problem, Jesus gave the solution. "For the law was given through Moses, but grace and truth came through Jesus Christ" (John 1:17).

Elijah was an outstanding figure in the Old Testament. He was a great prophet and his appearance with Moses on the Mount of Transfiguration testified that Jesus fulfilled the prophets, as well as the law.

The voice of God the Father gave further confirmation of the calling and the Sonship of Jesus. He acknowledged that Jesus had pleased him in the things he had said and done.

The Transfiguration is significant because:

1. The Transfiguration was the glorification of the body of Jesus. Those with him saw Jesus in his glory.

2. The appearance of Moses and Elijah testified that Jesus was the one of whom the law and the prophets spoke.
3. The approving testimony of God the Father further confirmed the identity of Jesus.

47. How Do We Know That Jesus Actually Healed People?

Many questions have arisen about the healing miracles of Jesus. Did he really heal people or were the cures self-induced? Can we believe the accounts given to us in the four Gospels? If he did heal, then how did he do it?

We will emphasize again that the accounts given to us in the four Gospels were eyewitness accounts of what transpired. The writers Matthew and John were there and saw what occurred. Mark and Luke are recording the eyewitness testimonies reported to them. The fact of the matter is that the miraculous healings were seen not only by the disciples but also by the multitudes. Among those who watched Jesus perform healings were the unbelieving religious leaders. Nowhere do we find them denying Jesus healed; we only find them questioning his authority.

But there are some who argue that the healing people received could have been self-induced. In the first century, before the advent of modern medicine, there was much ignorance regarding disease. Could not one easily argue that the healings of Jesus were self-induced because the illnesses were psychological rather than physical?

A study of the Gospel accounts will put that question to rest. The healing miracles of Jesus were of such a nature as to be beyond any natural explanation. For example, Jesus healed a man who was paralyzed (Mark 2:3-12) and another who was blind from birth (John 9:1-7). Lazarus was dead four days when Jesus brought him back to life (John 11). A young girl who was dead was brought back to life by Jesus (Luke 8:51-56). He healed ten lepers at once (Luke 17:11-19) and healed a man who was a deaf mute (Mark 7:31-37). It stretches beyond the bounds of imagination to think all these people, including the ones who had been dead, could only be ill in their minds and not in their bodies. We are never told of Jesus ever refusing to heal a person. And unless one would want to argue that no legitimate disease was present at his time, it seems clear that his healings were often and varied enough to prove valid.

48. Why Did Jesus Heal People?

The four Gospels testify that during the ministry of Jesus, multitudes of people were healed. "Now at evening, when the sun had set, they brought to Him all who were sick and those who were demon-possessed. And the whole city was gathered together at the door. Then He healed many who were sick with various diseases, and cast out many demons" (Mark 1:32-34). The question arises, why did Jesus go about healing people?

We can give at least two reasons why Jesus healed people. First it showed that he had power and authority, unlike anyone else. Jesus said this authority had been given to him by God the Father. The healing miracles were signs that God was with him and was authenticating his mission. These miraculous signs were displayed to demonstrate the authority of the Son.

They were not, however, to be an end in themselves. After Jesus healed the people referred to in this passage, the healings created quite a stir. Simon Peter and some others found Jesus the next morning in a deserted place and said, " 'Everyone is looking for You.' But He said to them, 'Let us go into the next towns, that I may preach there also, because for this purpose I have come forth' " (Mark 1:37, 38). Thus, the healing miracles were to substantiate his preaching. His primary mission was not to heal but to preach the kingdom of God.

We must not overlook another reason for Jesus' healing—his love and compassion for mankind. When sin entered the world, sickness, sorrow, and death came with it. While he was here on earth Jesus demonstrated his compassion for humanity by healing various ills. Time and time again the Gospels tell us that Jesus was moved with compassion when he saw sickness. He hated the suffering that he saw. His coming to earth was for the purpose of doing something about it. Jesus' death on the cross provided an answer for sin and its effects. The Bible testifies of a day when all sickness will be done away with. "And God will wipe away every tear from their eyes; there shall be no more death, nor sorrow, nor crying; and there shall be no more pain, for the former things have passed away" (Rev. 21:4).

In summing up, we can say that Jesus healed as a sign to the people that he was their Messiah. The healing miracles gave further credibility to his message. He also healed because he had compassion on the multitudes and their suffering. In all of this, Jesus showed his love and concern for mankind.

49. Why Did Jesus Tell the Leper to Keep Quiet about His Healing?

There is an event in the life of Jesus that some have difficulty in understanding. Jesus healed a man from leprosy and then told the man to keep silent to the multitude about his healing.

"Then a leper came to Him, imploring Him, kneeling down to Him and saying to Him, 'If You are willing, You can make me clean.' And Jesus, moved with compassion, put out His hand and touched him, and said to him, 'I am willing; be cleansed.' As soon as He had spoken, immediately the leprosy left him, and he was cleansed. And He strictly warned him and sent him away at once. And He said to him, 'See that you say nothing to anyone; but go your way, show yourself to the priest, and offer for your cleansing those things which Moses commanded, as a testimony to them.' But he went out and began to proclaim it freely, and to spread the matter, so that Jesus could no longer openly enter the city, but was outside in deserted places; and they came to Him from every quarter" (Mark 1:40-45).

If Jesus came to earth to proclaim himself as the Messiah, why would he want to keep a matter like this secret? Wasn't each miracle he performed a testimony that he was the Messiah? Why the desire for silence?

Some have said that Jesus told the man to be silent because he did not want people to perceive him only as a "healer." Others contend Jesus did not want the large crowds that a miracle like this would draw.

But the most reasonable answer is not that Jesus wanted the healing to be kept secret. Jesus wanted the man to first fulfill the requirements of the law. In Leviticus 14:2-8 God had prescribed the ritual for lepers that had been cleansed. The process included a number of steps before the man could be declared healed and allowed to return to the temple for worship. Jesus knew the law and testified that he came to fulfill the law. "Do not think that I came to destroy the Law or the Prophets. I did not come to destroy but to fulfill" (Matt. 5:17). Jesus' request was not a desire for the miracle to be silenced but a desire to see the law of God fulfilled. Moreover, the priests, to whom the leper was to show himself, were the people who were rejecting Jesus' claim to be the Messiah. This healing would be another testimony to them.

50. In What Ways Did Jesus Demonstrate His Authority?

As the Son of God, Jesus exercised authority over all realms. The Gospel of Matthew relates the different areas over which Jesus demonstrated his authority.

Incurable disease. After delivering the Sermon on the Mount Jesus came down from the mountain and reached out to the most repulsive of people, a man with leprosy. At this time there was no known cure for the disease. A leper was considered unclean and his life was a living death. Jesus had compassion on this particular man and healed him instantaneously. "And behold, a leper came and worshiped Him, saying, 'Lord, if You are willing, You can make me clean.' Then Jesus put out His hand and touched him, saying, 'I am willing; be cleansed.' And immediately his leprosy was cleansed" (Matt. 8:2, 3). Here Jesus demonstrated authority over the realm of incurable disease.

Healing from a distance. Jesus had the ability to heal someone without being present. A centurion approached Jesus on behalf of his paralyzed servant. The centurion's faith was such that he believed the servant would be healed if Jesus just gave the word; there was no need for his actual presence. Jesus marveled at the man's faith. "When Jesus heard it, He marveled, and said to those who followed, 'Assuredly, I say to you, I have not found such great faith, not even in Israel!' . . . Then Jesus said to the centurion, 'Go your way; and as you have believed, so let it be done for you.' And his servant was healed that same hour" (Matt. 8:10, 13). Jesus exhibited power to heal when he was not present, not even near the afflicted person.

Nature is under his authority. Jesus is not only the Lord over disease, he is also the Lord over nature. A great storm arose on the sea covering the boat with the waves. "Then His disciples came to Him and awoke Him, saying, 'Lord, save us! We are perishing!' But He said to them, 'Why are you fearful, O you of little faith?' Then He arose and rebuked the winds and the sea. And there was a great calm. And the men marveled, saying, 'Who can this be, that even the winds and the sea obey Him?' " (Matt. 8:25-27). Jesus displayed authority over nature.

Over the supernatural. Jesus also had authority over the supernatural realm. Jesus met two demon-possessed men who were terrorizing the countryside. When Jesus approached they cried out, "What have we to do with You, Jesus, You Son of God? Have You come here to torment us before the time?" (Matt. 8:29). Jesus cast out the demons into a herd of swine and the two men returned to normalcy. By doing this Jesus showed authority in the area of the supernatural.

Authority over life and death. The final area over which Jesus demonstrated his authority was over life and death. "While He spoke these things to them, behold, a ruler came and worshiped Him, saying, 'My daughter has just died, but come and lay Your hand on her and she will live.' . . . And when Jesus came into the ruler's house, and saw the flute players and the noisy crowd wailing, He said to them, 'Make room, for the girl is not dead, but sleeping.' And they laughed Him to scorn. But when the crowd was put outside, He went in and took her by the hand, and the girl arose" (Matt. 9:18, 23-25). Even death was subject to his authority.

Jesus showed that he has authority:
1. Over incurable disease.
2. To heal from a distance.
3. To command and control nature.
4. Over the supernatural.
5. Over life and death.

By doing these things Jesus demonstrated clearly that he is Lord of all.

51. Did the People in Jesus' Time Deny His Miraculous Deeds?

Many people since the time of Christ have denied his miracles. For whatever reason, they have not believed the New Testament's account of his supernatural works. The people living in Jesus' day, however, had a chance to witness firsthand whether or not he performed miraculous deeds. They had a lot to say on the matter.

First it must be recognized that the people living at the time of Jesus were as skeptical of the miraculous as modern man. There was no consensus of opinion that the miracles, such as the New Testament reports, were understandable occurrences. One need only look at the responses by the people to the miracles of Jesus to see that this is the case.

When Jesus healed a man who had been blind from birth, the response was amazement: "Since the world began it has been unheard of that anyone opened the eyes of one who was born blind" (John 9:32). They were not used to seeing something like this. The feat was something extraordinary to them.

On another occasion, Jesus healed a man who had been lame all of his life. When he performed this deed the people reacted as anyone would: "And immediately he arose, took up the bed, and went out in the presence of them all, so that all were amazed and glorified God, saying, 'We never saw anything like this!' " (Mark 2:12).

On the Sea of Galilee Jesus performed a miracle like no one had ever seen: "And a windstorm came down on the lake, and they were filling with water, and were in jeopardy. And they came to him and awoke Him, saying, 'Master, Master, we are perishing!' Then He arose and rebuked the wind and the raging of the water. And they ceased, and there was a calm. But He said to them, 'Where is your faith?' And they were afraid, and marveled, saying to one another, 'Who can this be? For He commands even the winds and water, and they obey Him!' " (Luke 8:23-25).

These accounts illustrate that first-century man was just as amazed and puzzled as modern man when it came to the miraculous. But we see that these same people, even though they were not used to seeing miracles, could not deny the deeds of Jesus.

The religious rulers, who were the enemies of Jesus, sought to discredit him. Instead of denying his miracles, they attributed them to the power of the Devil. "Then one was brought to Him who was demon-possessed, blind and mute; and He healed him, so that the blind and mute man both spoke and saw. And all the multitudes were amazed and said, 'Could this be the Son of David?' But when the Pharisees heard it they said, 'This fellow does not cast out demons except by Beelzebub, the ruler of the demons' " (Matt. 12:22-24).

On the day of Pentecost, after the death, resurrection, and ascension of Jesus, Simon Peter, in testifying to Christ's resurrection, appealed to the knowledge of his hearers. "Men of Israel, hear these words: Jesus of Nazareth, a Man attested by God to you by miracles, wonders, and signs which God did through Him in your midst, as you yourselves also know" (Acts

2:22). He stated to that large audience that the miracles of Jesus were something that they knew about. The fact that Peter was not immediately shouted down demonstrates that the people knew he was telling the truth. Multitudes had seen Jesus perform many miracles. The certainty that Jesus performed miracles was never in question. The question was, how did he do them?

The religious leaders, by arguing that Christ's miracles were a work of Satan, were acknowledging the fact that Jesus was a miracle worker. If they could have denied them, they would have, but the lack of denial on their part shows, from an unfriendly source, that the miracles attributed to Jesus did occur.

52. Did Jesus Break the Sabbath?

The issue that marked the break between Jesus and the religious rulers was the Sabbath. After Jesus healed a man with a withered hand on the Sabbath, the outraged religious leaders plotted to kill him. "Then the Pharisees went out and took counsel against Him, how they might destroy Him" (Matt. 12:14).

Why did this healing on the Sabbath offend them so much? What was so special about the Sabbath that caused this outrage?

The Sabbath was the focus of the fourth of the Ten Commandments God had given to Moses for the nation Israel. "Remember the Sabbath day, to keep it holy" (Exod. 20:8). The Sabbath began on Friday at sundown and ended at sundown on Saturday. It was the one day during the week when the people were supposed to cease from their labors in order to honor God.

During the history of the Israelite people, however, the religious authorities tacked on many man-made commandments concerning the Sabbath. There were all sorts of rules stating what a person could and could not do. By the time Jesus came, the observance of the Sabbath was more mechanical than spiritual. Jesus exposed the hypocrisy of the man-made rules through several incidents that happened on the Sabbath.

"At that time Jesus went through the grain fields on the Sabbath. And His disciples were hungry, and began to pluck heads of grain and to eat. But when the Pharisees saw it, they said to Him, 'Look, Your disciples are doing what is not lawful to do on the Sabbath!' Then He said to them, 'Have you not read what David did when he was hungry, he and those who were with him: how he entered the house of God and ate the showbread which was not lawful for him to eat, nor for those who were with him, but only for the priests? Or have you not read in the law that on the Sabbath the priests in the temple profane the Sabbath, and are blameless? But I say to you that in this place there is One greater than the temple. But if you had known what this means, "I desire mercy and not sacrifice," you would not have condemned the guiltless. For the Son of Man is Lord even of the Sabbath' " (Matt. 12:1-8).

Jesus was pointing out that the attitude, which had developed concerning the Sabbath, was in error. As he clearly told them, "The Sabbath was made for man, and not man for the Sabbath" (Mark 2:27). Therefore, Jesus did not break the Sabbath but observed it the way God had intended it to be observed.

Jesus' stressing of his authority as the Lord of all, including the Sabbath, was more than the hypocritical religious leaders could bear and caused them to plot his death. But the sin lay with the religious leaders who had perverted the observance and the meaning of the Sabbath that God had given them.

53. Why Did Jesus Tell His Disciples to Preach Only to the Nation Israel?

Early in his ministry Jesus sent his disciples throughout the land of Israel to preach the message of the kingdom of God. When he sent them out, he commanded that they preach only to Jews and not to Gentiles (non-Jews) or Samaritans (half-Jews). "Do not go into the way of the Gentiles, and do not enter a city of the Samaritans. But go rather to the lost sheep of the house of Israel. And as you go, preach, saying, 'The kingdom of heaven is at hand' " (Matt. 10:5-7). Why were they not allowed to preach to anyone but the Jews?

The biblical reason that Jesus' disciples went only to the Jews was to fulfill the Old Testament promises of God. According to Scripture, the people of Israel were to be the first to hear the message of the kingdom of God. Jesus had come as their Messiah. He and his disciples proclaimed that the kingdom which had been predicted in the Old Testament was now at hand. Jesus was the Jews' rightful King and, as King, he was sending his messengers to announce his kingdom.

It is not that the kingdom would be exclusively Jewish. Jesus had promised the inclusion of non-Jews. Once, after seeing the faith of a Roman centurion, Jesus remarked, "Assuredly, I say to you, I have not found such great faith, not even in Israel! And I say to you that many will come from east and west, and sit down with Abraham, Isaac, and Jacob in the kingdom of heaven" (Matt. 8:10, 11).

We see in this instance that Jesus was sending out his disciples, to the Jews, to fulfill the various Old Testament prophecies of a Messiah coming to Israel. Yet this was only the beginning. After his message went to Israel, the whole world was to hear it. Jesus later would tell his disciples, "Go therefore and make disciples of all the nations" (Matt. 28:19). Consequently when the disciples were told to go to the Jews and not the non-Jews, it was a matter of fulfilling God's promises in the proper order.

54. Did Jesus Know the People Would Reject Him?

When Christ came and preached the kingdom of God to the nation Israel his message was rejected. He was brought to Pilate for crucifixion by the religious leaders because they believed him to be a blasphemer. "We have a law, and according to our law He ought to die, because He made Himself the Son of God" (John 19:7). Although some had believed in him, the nation as a whole rejected him.

Did Christ know this would occur? Was he aware that his message would not be heeded? If so, then was his offer of the kingdom a legitimate one?

The two comings of Christ were predicted in the Old Testament. The prophets spoke of both his suffering and his glory. At his first coming he was to suffer for the sins of the world. Jesus was well aware of what would happen to him. He knew that his message would be rejected.

At the beginning of his public ministry Jesus spoke of both his death and resurrection. "So the Jews answered and said to Him, 'What sign do You show to us, since You do these things?' Jesus answered and said to them, 'Destroy this temple, and in three days I will raise it up' . . . But he was speaking of the temple of His body. Therefore, when He had risen from the dead, His disciples remembered that He had said this to them" (John 2:18, 19, 21-22). From the beginning of his ministry Jesus was well aware that the people would reject him.

Does this make his offer of a kingdom illegitimate? No. When Jesus came the first time, he promised the people that God's kingdom would take place if they believed in him. He knew they were going to reject him but that did not make his offer invalid. If the people would have believed in him, God's kingdom would have been established then and there. The offer was legitimate. But he knew they would not believe.

Though the rightful king was crucified He has promised to come again for those who believe in Him and judge those who do not.

55. How Did Jesus Fulfill the Law of Moses?

The law that God gave to Moses for the people Israel was a central part of their existence. It was the perfect standard by which they were to conduct their lives. Though the law was perfect, it revealed how imperfect each individual was. The law gave people the knowledge of sin but not the solution. "Therefore by the deeds of the law no flesh will be justified in His sight, for by the law is the knowledge of sin" (Rom. 3:20).

Everyone fell short of the requirements and standards the law established.

Jesus, as the promised Messiah, came and fulfilled the law of Moses. He testified, "Do not think that I came to destroy the Law or the Prophets. I did not come to destroy but to fulfill" (Matt. 5:17). Jesus is the only person who has ever kept the law perfectly. He did everything the law required, never once breaking any of its commandments.

Because he was sinless, Jesus was able to meet the requirements of the law to be the perfect sacrifice. His death redeemed mankind from the curse of the law. "Christ has redeemed us from the curse of the law, having become a curse for us (for it is written, 'Cursed is everyone who hangs on a tree')" (Gal. 3:13). The curse that the law had over mankind was now removed.

The death of Christ meant that those who were previously slaves under the law could now become children of God and heirs to his promises. "God sent forth His Son . . . to redeem those who were under the law, that we might receive the adoption as sons. And because you are sons, God has sent forth the Spirit of his Son into your hearts, crying out, 'Abba, Father!' Therefore you are no longer a slave but a son, and if a son, then an heir of God through Christ" (Gal. 4:4-7). Christ has taken away the bondage of the law for the believer and given him freedom.

How did Jesus fulfill the law of Moses?

1. Jesus is the only person who has ever lived who has perfectly kept God's law.
2. Because he fulfilled the law, Jesus was able to become the perfect sacrifice for sin.
3. Those who put their faith in him are freed from the bondage of the law and have become God's children.

56. Did Jesus Sidestep the Question of His Authority?

Jesus made it clear to the people that he knew who he was, where he had come from and what authority he had. On one occasion, however, he did not directly answer the question of his authority. But it was not to sidestep the matter. Matthew records what transpired.

"Now when He came into the temple, the chief priests and the elders of the people confronted Him as He was teaching, and said, 'By what authority are You doing these things? And who gave You this authority?' But Jesus answered and said to them, 'I also will ask you one thing, which if you tell Me, I likewise will tell you by what authority I do these things: The baptism of John, where was it from? From heaven or from men?' And they reasoned among themselves, saying, 'If we say, "From heaven," He will say to us, "Why then did you not believe him?" But if we say, "From men," we fear the multitude, for all count John as a prophet.' So they answered Jesus and said, 'We do not know.' And He said to them, 'Neither will I tell you by what authority I do these things' " (Matt. 21:23-27).

It must be remembered that two days before this exchange took place Jesus rode into Jerusalem on a donkey, accepting worship as the Messiah. Now the religious leaders wanted to know who gave him the authority to do that. But their question was hypocritical. For three years he had been telling them that his authority came from God the Father. Furthermore, he demonstrated every conceivable miracle to show he was the Messiah. But the religious leaders refused to believe his testimony.

Now again they asked the same question that they had asked three years before when Jesus first came to the temple: "What sign do You show to us, since You do these things?" (John 2:18). He had answered the question on that occasion and many times after that. Instead of answering it again, he countered with a question they could not answer. They refused to believe that John the Baptist was from God but they also refused to denounce him publicly. If any Jews should know the answer to this question, it was these religious leaders. Since they refused to answer Jesus' question, he refused to answer theirs.

This was not lack of conviction, doubt, or a sidestep on the part of Jesus. These people had made up their minds regarding him and they did not really want to know the answer to their question. Jesus, realizing their hypocrisy, chose not to answer them. Instead, he asked them a crucial question that they refused to answer.

57. Why Did Jesus Speak in Parables?

One of the methods Jesus employed in communicating his message was through parables. A parable is basically an earthly story with a heavenly meaning. When Jesus started telling parables to the people, his disciples asked the obvious question, "Why do You speak to them in parables?" (Matt. 13:10).

Jesus' answer to this question was quite revealing: "Because it has been given to you to know the mysteries of the kingdom of heaven, but to them it has not been given. . . . And in them the prophecy of Isaiah is fulfilled, which says: 'Hearing you will hear and shall not understand, and seeing you will see and not perceive; for the heart of this people has grown dull. Their ears are hard of hearing, and their eyes they have closed, lest they should see with their eyes and hear with their ears, lest they should understand with their heart and turn, so that I should heal them' " (Matt. 13:11, 14, 15).

Unwillingness on the part of the people to receive Jesus' message of the kingdom was the reason that he taught in parables. The truths of the kingdom of God were heard by them but not understood. It was not because God was hiding the truth from them—it was because they did not want to hear.

This points to a great truth. God had given the people every chance to accept the message of Jesus. His ministry was attested by miracles. He offered the proper credentials as the Messiah, yet they did not believe. The realities of the kingdom, therefore, were not theirs to know. The people who believed in Jesus as the Messiah would understand the parables, and hence, the great truths of the kingdom of God.

Some years later, the Apostle Paul would echo this same truth: "But we speak the wisdom of God in a mystery, the hidden wisdom which God ordained before the ages for our glory, which none of the rulers of this age knew; for had they known, they would not have crucified the Lord of glory. . . . For what man knows the things of a man except the spirit of the man which is in him? Even so no one knows the things of God except the Spirit of God. . . . But the natural man does not receive the things of the Spirit of God, for they are foolishness to him; nor can he know them, because they are spiritually discerned" (1 Cor. 2:7, 8, 11, 14).

The truth of God is to be understood spiritually. The great majority of the people in Jesus' day were not interested in God's truth. Jesus clearly said, "Therefore I speak to them in parables, because seeing they do not see, and hearing they do not hear, nor do they understand" (Matt. 13:13).

58. What Do the Parables of Jesus Tell Us about the Kingdom of God?

Jesus was asked by his disciples as to why he spoke in parables. He replied, "Because it has been given to you to know the mysteries of the kingdom of heaven, but to them it has not been given" (Matt. 13:11).

It is to those who have faith in him that the mysteries of the kingdom have been given. The mysteries of the kingdom tell us what to expect during this time of Jesus' absence from earth. They explain what will take place from tne time of Christ's ascension into heaven until he returns again. Four of the parables which Jesus gave are particularly illustrative of what will occur.

Varied Reception. In the parable of the sower (Matt. 13:1-23) Jesus told of a sower walking through a field and spreading seed. The seed fell upon four different kinds of soil representing the different responses that would be given to the message of Jesus. Some would not receive it at all, others would respond immediately to the message but would soon fall away. A third group would receive the message outwardly but would let the cares and concerns of this world system take control over their lives. There would be some, however, who would believe and make a genuine commitment to Christ. These believers would continue in their faith and each would produce good works that would testify to their commitment.

Counterfeit believers. The second parable Jesus gave is that of the wheat and tares (Matt. 13:24-30, 36-43). He gave this as a warning. True believers would coexist with counterfeit believers. Therefore, we can expect to see both individuals and organizations arise in the name of Christianity that do not believe in Jesus. From these individuals we can expect both words and deeds that are inconsistent with the example of Christ. This will continue until Christ comes again. At that time he will separate the wheat from the tares, that is, the true believers from the counterfeit.

Unnatural growth. The parable of the mustard seed (Matt. 13:31, 32) teaches that the cause of Christ would experience an unnatural growth. In the parable a huge tree results from the mustard seed rather than the plant it is supposed to become. In the same manner the church got involved in much more than God had intended. In the fourth century A.D., the Roman emperor Constantine "Christianized" the empire. The church and state merged causing all sorts of religious/political organizations to develop. Those who identified with Christianity were many, but genuine believers were a much smaller percentage. The mustard seed parable warns us of this unnatural growth.

A continued falling away. The parable of the leaven (Matt. 13:33) is one of the most important of all parables, for it illustrates a central Christian truth. Leaven is generally used as a symbol of evil. In this parable, the leaven, or false teaching, is introduced into the Christian community until the entire system is contaminated. This refers to the end times when professing Christianity will be all form and no substance. The majority of the professing Christians, though outwardly acknowledging Christ, will be spiritually dead. The closer we get to the second coming of Christ, we should expect to see more people falling away from the faith.

These four parables illustrate the course of the present age. Christ was telling believers what they should expect.

1. The message of Jesus will result in four different responses from those who hear it. Some will ignore it. Others will have an immediate response but will soon fall by the wayside. Still others will believe but they will let the concerns of this world override any commitment they have to Christ. Only one group will receive the word and continue on in faith. Their commitment to Christ will last and the result will be observable.

2. During the interval between Christ's first and second coming, the Devil will put people within the structure of the organized church. They will teach and do things contrary to Christ. At the second coming Christ will separate these counterfeit believers from the genuine ones.

3. The church will experience abnormal growth during its history. This occurred when the church and state merged making Christianity the state religion. It resulted in a great number of professing believers but a much smaller number of true believers.

4. Evil will contaminate the church to the place where professing Christianity will be corrupt. As we move closer toward the second coming of Christ, we should expect to see the visible church move farther away from the truth of God.

These four parables of Jesus give believers an idea of what things they should expect until he comes again. The course of this present age has gone exactly as Jesus predicted.

59. Why Did the Religious Leaders Accuse Jesus of Gluttony?

When Jesus was preaching the kingdom of God the religious leaders did not accept his authority. They accused him of many things such as lying, being energized by Satan, and being an illegitimate child. Among the numerous accusations was the claim that Jesus was a glutton.

Jesus made reference to the charge of the religious leaders: "For John came neither eating nor drinking and they say, 'He has a demon.' The Son of Man came eating and drinking, and they say, 'Look, a gluttonous man and a winebibber, a friend of tax collectors and sinners?' But wisdom is justified by her children" (Matt. 11:18, 19).

The Gospels record that Jesus frequently dined with people. He ate with tax collectors and others who would be considered sinners. Jesus explained the reason he did this: "Those who are well do not need a physician, but those who are sick. I have not come to call the righteous, but sinners, to repentance" (Luke 5:29-32).

Jesus moved among sinners because his message of salvation was to those who had sinned. He had come to seek and save the lost. For this he was accused of being a glutton. The problem is that the Pharisees could not be satisfied. John the Baptist arrived living the life of self-denial, neither eating or drinking with friends or at banquets. For doing this, the religious leaders accused him of being demonic. Jesus joined in with the feasting and he was labeled a glutton. Unbelief is never satisfied. The religious leaders, in their pride and arrogance, could not see that their sin was worse than those with whom Jesus mingled.

60. What Was the Leaven of the Pharisees and Sadducees That Jesus Warned Against?

Leaven is a substance, such as yeast, that is used to produce fermentation. This term is sometimes used in the Bible as a reference to sin. One of the warnings that Jesus gave his disciples was to beware of the leaven of the Pharisees and Sadducees.

After Jesus had fed the four thousand people with a few loaves and fish, the Pharisees came to him seeking a sign. He had already performed numerous miracles in their presence but they hypocritically came to him and asked for a sign. After rebuking them, Jesus left with his disciples. It is at this point that he made this statement about the leaven: " 'Take heed and beware of the leaven of the Pharisees and Sadducees.' And they reasoned among themselves, saying, 'It is because we have taken no bread.' But when Jesus perceived it, He said to them, . . . 'How is it you do not understand that I did not speak to you concerning bread?—but you should beware of the leaven of the Pharisees and Sadducees.' Then they understood that He did not tell them to beware of the leaven of bread, but of the doctrine of the Pharisees and Sadducees" (Matt. 16:6-8, 11, 12).

The Pharisees were a Jewish party that held to the strict interpretation of the Mosaic law. They were careful to obey the commandments down to the minutest detail, but their outward show of holiness only concealed their inward hypocrisy. Jesus made it clear that the leaven of the Pharisees referred to hypocrisy. "Beware of the leaven of the Pharisees, which is hypocrisy" (Luke 12:1).

Jesus used his sharpest language against the Pharisees: "Woe to you, scribes and Pharisees, hypocrites! For you are like whitewashed tombs which indeed appear beautiful outwardly, but inside are full of dead men's bones and all uncleanness. Even so you also outwardly appear righteous to men, but inside are full of hypocrisy and lawlessness" (Matt. 23:27, 28).

The Sadducees were a Jewish party that were opponents of the Pharisees. They were fewer in number than the Pharisees but were wealthy and well-educated. They had members among the priesthood and the Sanhedrin (the highest court and council of the Jews). The Sadducees, though part of the religious establishment, denied things supernatural. Their teaching was also to be avoided.

The harshest words of condemnation that Scripture records are those of Jesus condemning the religious leaders for their hypocrisy. They were supposed to be spiritual examples for the people, yet for all their outward show, inwardly they were corrupt. What made matters worse was that they believed themselves to be righteous.

61. Why Did Jesus Allow His Friend Lazarus to Die?

During Jesus' time on earth he healed many people of their sicknesses and diseases. But in one instance he allowed his sick friend, Lazarus, to die. Why did he do this? The account of Jesus raising Lazarus contains an insightful lesson regarding the ways of God.

Lazarus, who lived in the city of Bethany, had taken sick. His sisters, who had seen Jesus perform great miracles, sent a message to him in order that he might heal his sick friend. When Jesus heard of Lazarus' sickness he replied, "This sickness is not unto death, but for the glory of God, that the Son of God may be glorified through it" (John 11:4). In those words we have Jesus' statement with regard to the purpose of Lazarus' illness.

Instead of immediately coming to his sick friend's side, Jesus remained for two more days in the place where he was. He then made an awesome statement: " 'Our friend Lazarus sleeps, but I go that I may wake him up.' Then his disciples said, 'Lord, if he sleeps he will get well.' However, Jesus spoke of his death, but they thought that he was speaking about taking rest in sleep. Then Jesus said to them plainly, 'Lazarus is dead. And I am glad for your sakes that I was not there, that you may believe' " (John 11:11-15). Thus, Jesus acknowledged Lazarus' death and predicted that he would bring Lazarus back from the dead.

When Jesus arrived in Bethany, Lazarus had been dead four

days. The people were in mourning. Martha, a sister of Lazarus, went out to meet Jesus and displayed great faith. "Lord, if You had been here, my brother would not have died. But even now I know that whatever You ask of God, God will give You" (John 11:21, 22). Jesus then told Martha her brother would rise again. He went over to the tomb of Lazarus and wept. The Jews seeing this wondered, "Could not this Man, who opened the eyes of the blind, also have kept this man from dying?" (John 11:37). Why did Jesus let Lazarus die?

The answer is given to us in the next moment. Jesus ordered the stone to be taken away from the tomb and with a loud voice commanded Lazarus to come forth. Then a miracle occurred. Lazarus came back from the dead as Jesus had predicted. This act caused amazement to all who witnessed it.

Everyone wanted Jesus to heal Lazarus but his refusal brought about even greater glory to God. He could have arrived in time and saved Lazarus from dying, but he chose to bring him back from the dead. By predicting the outcome ahead of time he gave further testimony of his authority.

62. Why Was Jesus Betrayed by Judas Iscariot?

One of the darkest moments in all of history is the betrayal of Jesus by one of his own disciples, Judas Iscariot.

When the disciples came to Jerusalem for the last time, Jesus made it clear that his death would be upcoming. "You know that after two days is the Passover, and the Son of Man will be delivered up to be crucified" (Matt. 26:2). Realizing this, Judas went to the chief priests and said, " 'What are you willing to give me if I deliver Him to you?' And they counted out to him thirty pieces of silver. So from that time he sought opportunity to betray Him" (Matt. 26:15, 16).

On the night when Jesus and the disciples celebrated the Last Supper, Judas plotted with the religious rulers to take them to Jesus in the Garden of Gethsemane. It was there in the garden that Jesus was betrayed and arrested.

Why did he do it? If Jesus clearly demonstrated that he was the Son of God, then why did one of his own disciples betray him?

There have been a number of views put forth to explain why Judas did this. One view says that Judas was foreordained as a traitor and could do nothing about it. Jesus knew from the beginning that Judas would betray him. He had said to his disciples, " 'But there are some of you who do not believe.' For Jesus knew from the beginning who they were who did not believe, and would betray Him" (John 6:64). But because Jesus knew ahead of time that Judas would betray him does not mean that he caused Judas to do it. Judas acted on his own accord. He was not just a pawn or puppet in God's hands.

Another view argues that Judas was a fanatical believer in Jesus who wanted to force his hand by betraying him. Handing Jesus over to the religious leaders would supposedly force him to set up his Messianic kingdom. But this view does not square with the facts. Judas asked the chief priests for money for the betrayal, which is hardly in keeping with such "pure" spiritual motives. Moreover, the Gospels refer to Judas as a thief and a betrayer. Hardly the designation one would expect for a fanatical believer.

Others have considered Judas a superpatriot who wanted to use Jesus as a means to revolt against their Roman oppressors. But this does not fit the facts for the reasons mentioned above. There is no indication that Judas had any other motive but greed.

This brings us to the likely explanation. Judas was a thief whose ambition was to have power and money. By aligning himself close to Jesus, Judas believed that he would receive a prominent place in the kingdom. When Jesus talked about dying, Judas realized the kingdom was not going to come immediately. Therefore, he gained what he could by betraying Jesus. Judas did not ever believe in Jesus. He never referred to Jesus as Lord but rather as "master" or "teacher." Judas is an example of one who follows Jesus for all the wrong reasons. Jesus gave Judas' epitaph: "The Son of Man is betrayed! It would have been good for that man if he had not been born" (Matt. 26:24).

63. What Did Jesus Mean When He Prayed, "If Possible, Remove This Cup from Me"?

When Jesus was in the Garden of Gethsemane, awaiting to be betrayed by Judas Iscariot, he prayed to his heavenly Father saying, "Father, if it is Your will, remove this cup from Me; nevertheless not My will, but Yours, be done" (Luke 22:42).

His prayer to the Father brings up many questions. What was the cup he was referring to ? Had Jesus changed his mind about dying? Was he afraid to face death on the cross?

The idea that Jesus was afraid to face physical death does not fit the facts. He had known from the beginning of his ministry that he was going to die by crucifixion and had spoken about it often to the multitudes. The fear of physical death was not the issue because the events surrounding his death showed that Christ was a willing victim.

Some have thought Jesus was afraid he might die there in Gethsemane. He was in agony while he was praying to the Father. "And being in agony, He prayed more earnestly. And His sweat became like great drops of blood falling down to the ground" (Luke 22:44). But this is not what he was referring to for he knew that he was to die on the cross.

The cup which Jesus was referring to was not the cup of physical suffering but rather the spiritual suffering he was to face on the cross. Jesus did more than die a physical death. God the Father placed the sins of the world upon him at Calvary's cross. He who knew no sin was made sin for us. We cannot comprehend all that this meant. The sinless Son of God was about to take the punishment and suffering due all of mankind. The awful thing for Jesus was that he was to bear our sins separated from the Father. For all eternity the Father and

Son had been together and now, for the first time, they would be separated spiritually. This led Jesus to ask if there was any other way within God's will that God would let it be done that way. Yet the will of the Father was most important. Because the Father allowed the Son to suffer it showed that there was no other way. It was God's will for Jesus to present himself as the sinless sacrifice.

Therefore, Jesus prayed not out of fear or doubt but out of the conviction to deal with sin in a manner pleasing to the Father. It pleased the Father to allow his Son to be made the sacrifice in order that we might have our sins forgiven. The Son willingly obeyed.

64. Why Did the Religious Leaders Want to Kill Jesus?

The New Testament records that the religious leaders hated Jesus to the point that they arrested him, tried him and brought him to Pilate for a sentence of death. What made them so angry at him that they wanted to see him dead?

There were several things about Jesus that infuriated the religious leaders. These included (1) the claims that he made; (2) the deeds that he did; (3) the people with whom he socialized; and (4) the lack of respect he had for their religious traditions. These four things caused outrage among the religious rulers.

The claims that he made. The claims that Jesus made infuriated the religious leaders. When Jesus claimed to be the Messiah it meant his authority outweighed their authority. The religious leaders did not believe his claims and were angry that some of the people did. They said, "Have any of the rulers or the Pharisees believed in Him? But this crowd that does not know the law is accursed" (John 7:48, 49). The religious leaders assumed that the belief of some of the crowd was due to ignorance. But the attention Jesus was getting brought out the leaders' hatred and jealousy.

The deeds that he did. The deeds of Jesus also angered the religious leaders. After seeing Jesus heal a demon-possessed man some of the multitude questioned if Jesus could be the Messiah. "And all the multitudes were amazed and said, 'Could this be the Son of David [Messiah]?' But when the Pharisees heard it they said, 'This fellow does not cast out demons except by Beelzebub, the ruler of the demons' " (Matt. 12:23, 24). The miracle was undeniable, for the man was blind and mute as well as demon-possessed. Rather than believe Jesus to be the Messiah, these religious rulers attributed Jesus' power to the Devil. Thus their "official" explanation was that Jesus' power came from Satan. This was another cause for which they wanted him dead.

The people with whom he socialized. The religious leaders were filled with pride and arrogance. They were particularly proud that they did not socialize with "sinners." They did not believe that the Messiah would socialize with such a crowd. When one Pharisee saw Jesus allow a woman to wash his feet, he said, "This man, if He were a prophet, would know who and what manner of woman this is who is touching Him, for she is a sinner" (Luke 7:39). Jesus noted their opinion of him. "The Son of Man came eating and drinking, and they say, 'Look, a gluttonous man and a winebibber, a friend of tax collectors and sinners!" (Matt. 11:19). The religious rulers believed themselves to be righteous by avoiding sinners. When Jesus kept company with these individuals, it infuriated the proud Pharisees and other religious rulers.

The lack of respect for their traditions. As much as anything, the lack of regard that Jesus had for their religious traditions incensed the religious leaders. These traditions, which they observed so minutely, were ignored by Jesus. He knew thay were man-made rules that had not come from God. And it was Jesus' disregard for their traditions concerning the Sabbath that caused the most outrage. God had commanded the

Sabbath to be a day of rest from labors and a time to worship him. The religious leaders added all types of restrictions to the Sabbath making it difficult, if not impossible, to observe.

Jesus was grieved and angry at the way they had perverted the Sabbath observance. He asked the religious leaders, " 'Is it lawful on the Sabbath to do good or to do evil, to save life or to kill?' But they kept silent. So . . . He . . . looked around at them with anger, being grieved by the hardness of their hearts" (Mark 3:4, 5). Jesus then healed a man in their presence. This healing on the Sabbath was more than they could endure. They concluded that the genuine Messiah would not dare do such a thing. Their response was immediate: "Then the Pharisees went out and immediately plotted with the Herodians against Him, how they might destroy Him" (Mark 3:6). They were convinced that Jesus had to die.

In summary we can say that the reasons the religious leaders wanted Jesus dead included:
1. The claims which he made. By claiming to be the Messiah, Jesus' authority would be greater than any of theirs. They did not want to accept his authority as some of the people had.
2. Jesus' miraculous deeds pointed to the truth of his claims. Because they did not want to believe his claims, his miracles were attributed to Satan. The miracles were another thing that angered them.
3. Jesus' continual socializing with sinners was an affront to their pride. They believed themselves righteous by avoiding such people. Jesus' conduct caused outrage among them.
4. The thing that probably angered them the most was Jesus' lack of respect for their man-made traditions. When Jesus claimed to be Lord over the Sabbath they determined then and there that he must die.

We see that it was not for anything godly or righteous that the religious leaders wanted Jesus put to death. It was their hypocrisy, pride, and arrogance that caused them to bring Jesus before Pilate to be crucified. They did not want to hear the truth of God.

65. Why Did Jesus Die on the Cross?

Scripture testifies to the fact that Jesus died on a cross after being betrayed to the religious rulers by one of his own disciples, Judas Iscariot. But the immediate reason Jesus died was because of the envy of the Jews. Pontius Pilate recognized this when the Jewish religious leaders brought Jesus to him. "Now at the feast the governor was accustomed to releasing to the multitude one prisoner whom they wished. And they had then a notorious prisoner called Barabbas. Therefore, when they had gathered together, Pilate said to them, 'Whom do you want me to release to you? Barabbas, or Jesus who is called Christ?' For he knew that because of envy they had delivered Him" (Matt. 27:15-18). Their envy toward Jesus was due to the fact that he had drawn a large following by claiming to be the Messiah. His miracles verified his claims. Jesus also criticized their corrupt religious system. Because of this, they decided to kill him.

There are more significant reasons, however, why Jesus died on Calvary's cross.

At his baptism, when John the Baptist saw Jesus coming, he said, "Behold! The Lamb of God who takes away the sin of the world!" (John 1:29). Jesus had come into the world for the purpose of dying on the cross. His death accomplished several things.

Paying the penalty for sin. The death of Christ was the payment for sin—the ransom paid to God to satisfy his holy demands. The Bible pictures man as a sinner who had rebelled against God. Christ's death on the cross paid the penalty for the sin of mankind. Jesus died in our place as our substitute, receiving the punishment that was due us.

The Bible says, "[Christ] was delivered up because of our offenses, and was raised because of our justification" (Rom.

4:25); "so Christ was offered once to bear the sins of many" (Heb. 9:28). Because of Christ's death, believers will not have to suffer eternally for their sins.

The penalty that Jesus paid for sin was not only for the human race, it was also for everything in our universe that had been marred by sin. "Because the creation itself also will be delivered from the bondage of corruption into the glorious liberty of the children of God" (Rom. 8:21). The death of Christ had far-reaching consequences.

The love of God. The death of Christ upon the cross also demonstrated that God loves sinful man. The Scripture speaks of his death as an act of love toward mankind. "For God so loved the world that He gave His only begotten Son, that whoever believes in Him should not perish but have everlasting life" (John 3:16); "But God demonstrates His own love toward us, in that while we were still sinners, Christ died for us" (Rom. 5:8). It was love that motivated Jesus to come to earth and die on the cross and take the punishment as our substitute.

An example to the believer. The Bible tells us the love of God that was demonstrated by Jesus should serve as an example for how we should treat one another. "A new commandment I give to you, that you love one another; as I have loved you, that you also love one another. By this all will know that you are My disciples, if you have love for one another" (John 13:34, 35).

Why did Jesus die on the cross?
1. Christ was put to death because of the hatred the religious leaders had for him.
2. His death on the cross paid the penalty for the sin of mankind.
3. His sacrifice also covered everything in the universe that had been affected by sin.
4. His death demonstrates God's abounding love toward us.

5. His sacrificial death provided an example to believers as to how we are to treat each other.

66. How Do Skeptics View the Death of Christ?

We have seen what the Scriptures say concerning Christ's death. We also need to consider some of the inadequate views that are brought forward to explain why he died.

His death was not, as some contend, merely an example of courage and loyalty to a particular cause. It was much more than that. His sacrificial act was not to prove some particular point or reveal how courageous he was, it was for the purpose of dying for the sins of the world. He was not a martyr. He chose to die.

There are those who contend that Jesus' death was immoral since he was an innocent victim, the just dying for the unjust. This view does not stand because Jesus, although innocent, was a willing substitute for the sin of man. This he made clear: "No one takes [My life] from Me, but I lay it down of Myself. I have power to lay it down, and I have power to take it again. This command I have received from My Father" (John 10:18). The Son was in full sympathy with the wishes of the Father.

Others believe the death of Christ was merely an example of how we should give ourselves on behalf of others. They argue that the death had no value in and of itself except to create a "moral effect." The Scriptures speak to the contrary. "Knowing that you were not redeemed with corruptible things, like silver or gold, from your aimless conduct received by tradition from your fathers, but with the precious blood of Christ, as of a lamb without blemish and without spot" (1 Pet. 1:18, 19).

Finally, there are those who teach that the death of Christ showed that his mission failed. They say, instead of Jesus setting up God's eternal kingdom as he was supposed to, he died, failing his assigned task. But nothing could be further from the truth. Before he came to earth Jesus knew that his message would be rejected and that he would die. "From that time Jesus began to show to His disciples that He must go to Jerusalem, and suffer many things from the elders and chief priests and scribes, and be killed, and be raised again the third day" (Matt. 16:21).

His sacrifice, rather than being a defeat, was a victory over the power of sin and death. It was for this purpose that Jesus came to earth.

67. What Does the Bible Mean When It Says Christ Redeemed Us?

As we study the life of Christ we often come into contact with the term *redemption*. The word *redeem* means "to purchase." When Christ died for our sins he paid the price for them with his own blood. Peter wrote, "Knowing that you were not redeemed with corruptible things, like silver or gold, from your aimless conduct received by tradition from your fathers, but with the precious blood of Christ, as of a lamb without blemish and without spot" (1 Pet. 1:18, 19). The Bible also speaks of Christ redeeming us from the law: "Christ has redeemed us from the curse of the law, having become a curse for us" (Gal. 3:13). What then does this mean?

The New Testament uses two terms that shed light upon the full meaning of redemption, *agorazo* and *lutro*.

The word *agorazo,* along with its variation *exagorazo,* has the idea of buying a slave out of the market and then taking him home. This term speaks of Christ buying us out of the slave market of the world. The price Jesus paid, with his own blood, was sufficient to buy every slave out of the market. His purchase also means that that slave would never be sold again. We have all been slaves to sin, and if we allow him to be our Master, then we need never be sold again, for he becomes our eternal Master.

The word *lutro* means "to buy and give freedom." When Christ bought us from the marketplace of the world, he not only gave us our freedom, he also made us part of his family. Those who receive by faith the benefits of the sacrifice Christ provided become the children of God, part of his eternal family. "The Spirit Himself bears witness with our spirit that we are children of God, and if children, then heirs—heirs of God and joint heirs with Christ, if indeed we suffer with Him, that we may also be glorified together" (Rom. 8:16, 17).

Redemption, properly understood, means:

1. Christ bought us out of the slave market of the world.
2. The price he paid was his own blood.
3. When he bought us, he gave us our freedom.
4. We cannot be sold again as slaves.
5. We have become part of his family and participants in his rightful inheritance.

All this is obtainable if we choose to place our faith in the sacrifice which he made on our behalf.

68. What Is the Significance of the Words Jesus Spoke While on the Cross?

The Gospels record that during the six hours Jesus was hanging on the cross he made seven different statements. These statements are of tremendous significance because they are the last words of Jesus before his death. They demonstrate that Jesus was consistent in his life and in his message until the end.

"Father, forgive them, for they do not know what they do" *(Luke 23:34).* This first of seven sayings of Jesus shows that he was thinking of others until the end of his life. Even while experiencing the horrible pain of crucifixion, he was praying for the very people who caused his suffering. He came to earth for the purpose of forgiving sinners and he loved them and forgave them up until the end. It was because of man's sin that he was on the cross—suffering on behalf of that sin.

"Today you will be with Me in Paradise" *(Luke 23:43).* Not only did Jesus forgive those who crucified him, he also forgave one of the thieves crucified next to him. When the thieves were put on the cross both of them cursed Jesus but, as time elapsed, one of the thieves had a change of heart. "Then

one of the criminals who were hanged blasphemed Him, saying, 'If You are the Christ, save Yourself and us.' But the other, answering, rebuked him, saying, 'Do you not even fear God, seeing you are under the same condemnation? And we indeed justly, for we receive the due reward of our deeds; but this Man has done nothing wrong.' Then he said to Jesus, 'Lord, remember me when You come into Your kingdom' " (Luke 23:39-42). It was at this juncture that Jesus made his second statement from the cross promising to forgive the repentant thief. Again we see Jesus' concern for others. His example later led the Apostle Paul to exhort the Philippian church, "Let nothing be done through selfish ambition or conceit, but in lowliness of mind let each esteem others better than himself" (Phil. 2:3).

"Woman, behold your son" (John 19:26). As Jesus continued to suffer on the cross his mind was still upon others. He saw his mother standing near to the Apostle John and said, "Woman, behold your son." He then looked at John and said, "Behold your mother!" By doing this he was entrusting the care of his mother to John. The law required the firstborn son to take care of his parents, and Jesus was obeying the law of God up until the end. Early in his ministry Jesus emphasized his respect for the law: "Do not think that I came to destroy the Law or the Prophets. I did not come to destroy but to fulfill" (Matt. 5:17). He honored and obeyed the law throughout his life and he also honored the law while suffering his death.

"My God, My God, why have You forsaken Me?" (Matt. 27:46). The fourth saying of Jesus from the cross is probably the most difficult for us to understand. The sinless Son of God who had been, from all eternity, in an intimate relationship with his Father, is now spiritually separated from him. When the sins of the world were put upon Jesus there was, for the first time, a separation between the Father and the Son. The Bible records that something happened between them that we can understand only through the eye of faith. "That is, that God

was in Christ reconciling the world to Himself" (2 Cor. 5:19). The Father was placing the sins of the world upon the Son in order that everything in the universe that had been affected by sin could again be made right with God. Jesus was suffering the pain and separation that we deserve. "For He made Him who knew no sin to be sin for us, that we might become the righteousness of God in Him" (2 Cor. 5:21). In order for this to occur, the Father had to forsake the Son and punish him on our behalf.

"I thirst!" (John 19:28). The fifth statement that Jesus made from the cross reminds us again that he suffered as a human being. The Bibles says, "After this, Jesus, knowing that all things were now accomplished, that the Scripture might be fulfilled, said, 'I thirst!' " (John 19:28). He lived as a man and suffered as a man in order that he could identify with suffering humanity. From this statement we observe that Jesus suffered the full physical effect of crucifixion. There was no easing up, for the weight of our sins was placed upon him.

"It is finished!" (John 19:30). The sixth statement from Jesus while upon the cross was a cry of victory. The Greek text reads *tetelestai,* "It is finished." What was finished? As we consider the life and ministry of Jesus we can think of several things that his death made complete.

First, Jesus had finished the task that the Father had sent him to earth to accomplish, namely to provide salvation for mankind. By living his entire life without sin, Jesus was able to become the perfect sacrifice for the sins of the world. The way of salvation had now been made complete. No more animal sacrifices were necessary for they had only pointed to the ultimate sacrifice Jesus had now offered. His was the supreme sacrifice which satisfied the righteous demands of a holy God.

The second thing that was accomplished by Jesus on the cross was the fulfillment of prophecy. The predicted Messiah had come as God promised he would. Prophecies of the Word of God, which are always accurate, had again come to pass.

The Savior was promised; now Christ the Savior had come and accomplished the promised salvation.

A third matter that was accomplished by Jesus' death on the cross was the victory over the Devil. The Scripture says that one of the purposes for Jesus' coming was to destroy the works of the Devil (1 John 3:8). The death of Christ finished that task. The dominion over the earth that man, through his sin, had handed over to the Devil was now won back. The authority of Satan had been vanquished, the victory had been won. When Christ comes again he will take hold of the victory that he won over the Devil on Calvary's cross.

A fourth and final reason that Jesus said "It is finished" is with regard to his own suffering. Jesus spent over thirty years upon the earth living among sinful man, suffering from the self-imposed limitations of that existence. He had now endured the final six hours of that life suffering on a cross. This was now finished. He would no longer have to suffer the limits of space and time. It was finished!

"Father, into Your hands I commend My spirit" (*Luke 23:46*). This is the final statement that we have from Jesus before his death. Everything had been completed and now it was time to dismiss his spirit. Jesus had previously made the statement that he would willingly lay down his life for his sheep. "Therefore My Father loves Me, because I lay down My life that I may take it again. No one takes it from Me, but I lay it down of Myself. I have power to lay it down, and I have power to take it again. This command I have received from My Father" (John 10:17, 18). From this we realize that Jesus had to purposely dismiss his spirit; it could not be taken from him. Unless he desired to die, he would not have had to. Because he was a willing victim, however, he chose to die. Upon making his final statement, Jesus died.

The seven statements Jesus made from the cross have far-reaching significance for us today. They once again remind us that his death, besides being a fact of history, was much more than that. It was the supreme sacrifice that secured our salvation. His final words show us that we can have the utmost confidence in him as our Savior.

69. Did Jesus Predict He Would Rise from the Dead?

One of the strongest pieces of evidence for the Resurrection is that it was predicted beforehand by Jesus. Rather than being an afterthought, the Resurrection was central to his ministry and message.

Early in his ministry when the Jews asked for a sign, Jesus gave the sign of the Resurrection: " 'Destroy this temple, and in three days I will raise it up.' Then the Jews said, 'It has taken forty-six years to build this temple, and will You raise it up in three days?' But He was speaking of the temple of His body. Therefore, when He had risen from the dead, His disciples remembered that He had said this to them" (John 2:19-22).

He later repeated his prediction: "An evil and adulterous generation seeks after a sign, and no sign will be given to it except the sign of the prophet Jonah. For as Jonah was three days and three nights in the belly of the great fish, so will the Son of Man be three days and three nights in the heart of the earth" (Matt. 12:39, 40). Therefore, according to Jesus, the Resurrection was to be the sign that proved him to be the Messiah.

After Simon Peter confessed Jesus to be the Messiah, Jesus began to emphasize his resurrection. "From that time Jesus began to show to His disciples that He must go to Jerusalem, and suffer many things from the elders and chief priests and scribes, and be killed, and be raised again the third day" (Matt. 16:21).

The predictions of the Resurrection were such common knowledge that the religious leaders asked for a guard at Jesus' tomb after his death. "On the next day, which followed the Day of Preparation, the chief priests and Pharisees gathered together to Pilate, saying, 'Sir, we remember, while He was still alive, how that deceiver said, "After three days I will rise." Therefore command that the tomb be made secure until the third day, lest His disciples come by night and steal Him away, and say to the people, "He has risen from the dead." So the last deception will be worse than the first' " (Matt. 27:62-64). However, the precautions taken did not stop Jesus from rising from the dead.

From these predictions it can be readily seen that the Resurrection was not an afterthought but a central part of the message of Jesus.

70. What Happened on the Day Jesus Rose from the Dead?

The Bible records events of the first Easter that show the Resurrection took the followers of Jesus by surprise. Luke writes:

"Now on the first day of the week, very early in the morning, they, and certain other women with them, came to the tomb bringing the spices which they had prepared. But they found the stone rolled away from the tomb. Then they went in and did not find the body of the Lord Jesus. And it happened, as they were greatly perplexed about this, that behold, two men stood by them in shining garments. Then, as they were afraid and bowed their faces to the earth, they said to them, 'Why do you seek the living among the dead? He is not here, but is risen! Remember how He spoke to you when He was still in Galilee, saying, "The Son of Man must be delivered into the hands of sinful men, and be crucified, and the third day rise again." ' And they remembered His words. Then they returned from the tomb and told all these things to the eleven and to all the rest" (Luke 24:1-9).

From this account, along with the testimony of the other three Gospels, we can determine the following things occurred on Easter Sunday before Jesus appeared to anyone:

1. The women came early in the morning to finish the anointing of the body of Jesus (Luke 24:1).
2. They knew that a huge stone was rolled in front of the

tomb and discussed among themselves how they could move it (Mark 16:3).

3. When they arrived at the tomb they found the guards had fallen in a dead faint and the stone was rolled away (Matt. 28:1-4).

4. When they looked inside the tomb they saw that the body of Jesus was gone (Luke 24:3).

5. The missing body surprised them. They were not expecting the body to be gone (Luke 24:4).

6. They encountered two angels, or messengers, who told them Christ had risen. The angels reminded them that Jesus predicted on the third day he would rise again (Luke 24:4-6).

7. This caught the women completely by surprise. They had gone to the tomb to anoint a dead man. But they did remember Jesus predicting his resurrection (Luke 24:8).

8. The women then returned and told the others what had happened (Luke 24:9).

9. At first the men did not believe the women's report but eventually decided to investigate for themselves (Luke 24:11).

10. When they arrived at the tomb they discovered the body gone but the graveclothes were still there. The handkerchief that had been placed around his head was not with the rest of the clothes but folded in a place by itself (John 20:6-8).

11. All these events bewildered the disciples but did not convince them that Jesus had risen. "For as yet they did not know the Scripture, that He must rise again from the dead" (John 20:9).

These are some of the things that transpired on the first Easter before Jesus appeared to anyone. The huge stone that was moved and the missing body caused confusion in the minds of the disciples. They were not expecting Jesus to rise from the dead even though he had predicted it. The separation of the graveclothes caused John to believe, but even he did not fully understand what was going on. One surprising event after another happened on that first Easter before Jesus' followers began to comprehend that Jesus was alive.

71. Did Anyone See Jesus after His Death?

All of Jesus' followers were surprised by the events that took place on that first Easter. The one happening that surprised them most, however, was seeing the risen Christ. The primary reason the disciples of Jesus believed in the Resurrection was that they actually saw Jesus after he was risen from the dead. Scripture testifies that over a forty-day period following the Resurrection, the disciples saw the risen Christ in a variety of different places and times. "To whom He also presented Himself alive after His suffering by many infallible proofs, being seen by them during forty days and speaking of the things pertaining to the kingdom of God" (Acts 1:3).

After the Resurrection Jesus was seen by many different people. The New Testament records that he appeared:

To Mary Magdalene. "Now when she had said this, she turned around and saw Jesus standing there, and did not know that it was Jesus. Jesus said to her, 'Woman, why are you weeping? Whom are you seeking?' She, supposing Him to be the gardener, said to Him, 'Sir, if You have carried Him away, tell me where You have laid Him, and I will take Him away.' Jesus said to her, 'Mary!' She turned and said to Him, 'Rabboni!' (which is to say, Teacher)" (John 20:14-16).

To the women returning from the empty tomb. "And as they went to tell His disciples, behold, Jesus met them, saying, 'Rejoice!' And they came and held Him by the feet and worshiped Him" (Matt. 28:9).

To the Apostle Peter. "The Lord is risen indeed, and has appeared to Simon!" (Luke 24:34).

To two disciples on the Emmaus Road. "Now behold, two of them were traveling that same day to a village called Emmaus, which was about seven miles from Jerusalem. . . . So it was, while they conversed and reasoned, that Jesus Himself drew near and went with them" (Luke 24:13-15).

To the disciples with Thomas absent. "Then, the same day at evening, being the first day of the week, when the doors were shut where the disciples were assembled, for fear of the Jews, Jesus came and stood in the midst, and said to them, 'Peace be with you.' Now when He had said this, He showed them His hands and His side. Then the disciples were glad when they saw the Lord" (John 20:19, 20).

To the disciples with Thomas present. "And after eight days His disciples were again inside, and Thomas with them. Jesus came, the doors being shut, and stood in the midst, and said, 'Peace to you!' Then He said to Thomas, 'Reach your finger here, and look at My hands; and reach your hand here, and put it into My side. Do not be unbelieving, but believing.' And Thomas answered and said to Him, 'My Lord and My God!' " (John 20:26-28).

To his disciples in Galilee. "Then the eleven disciples went away into Galilee, to the mountain which Jesus had appointed for them. And when they saw Him, they worshiped Him" (Matt. 28:16, 17).

To seven disciples on the Sea of Tiberias. "After these things Jesus showed Himself again to the disciples at the Sea of Tiberias" (John 21:1).

Again to the eleven disciples. "Afterward He appeared to the eleven as they sat at the table; and He rebuked their unbelief and hardness of heart, because they did not believe those who had seen Him after He had risen" (Mark 16:14).

To over five hundred people at one time. "After that He was seen by over five hundred brethren at once, of whom the greater part remain to the present, but some have fallen asleep" (1 Cor. 15:6).

To James. "After that He was seen by James" (1 Cor. 15:7).

When he ascended into heaven. "Now when He had spoken these things, while they watched, He was taken up, and a cloud received Him out of their sight" (Acts 1:9).

These are some of the appearances that Jesus made over the forty-day period from his resurrection to ascension. After his ascension he appeared again.

To Saul of Tarsus. "And as he journeyed he came near Damascus, and suddenly a light shone around him from heaven. Then he fell to the ground, and heard a voice saying to him, 'Saul, Saul, why are you persecuting Me?' And he said, 'Who are You, Lord?' And the Lord said, 'I am Jesus, whom you are persecuting' " (Acts 9:3-5).

To the Apostle John on the Isle of Patmos. "I was in the Spirit on the Lord's Day, and I heard behind m e a loud voice, as of a trumpet, saying, 'I am the Alpha and the Omega, the First and the Last" (Rev. 1:10, 11).

These appearances of Jesus convinced his disciples and Paul that he had truly risen from the dead. They testified time and again of what they had seen and heard. "That which was from the beginning, which we have heard, which we have seen with our eyes, which we have looked upon, and our hands have handled, concerning the Word of life" (1 John 1:1).

Simon Peter told an audience in Jerusalem, "But you denied the Holy One and the Just, and asked for a murderer to be granted to you, and killed the Prince of life, whom God raised from the dead, of which we are witnesses" (Acts 3:14, 15).

The disciples also showed that they knew the difference between myth and reality. "For we did not follow cunningly devised fables when we made known to you the power and coming of our Lord Jesus Christ, but were eyewitnesses of His majesty" (2 Pet. 1:16).

Thus we see them testifying time and time again to the fact that they were eyewitnesses. This firsthand evidence that the disciples recorded is a powerful argument for the resurrection of Christ. The disciples knew that he had risen because they saw him with their own eyes.

72. What Indirect Evidence Is There for the Resurrection?

We have already observed that the direct testimony of the disciples to Christ's resurrection is a powerful argument that it took place. This is known as eyewitness or firsthand testimony. There is another type of testimony that comes into play that gives further reason to believe that Christ has risen. This is indirect or circumstantial evidence.

At least three lines of indirect evidence can be offered to further bolster the case for the Resurrection: (1) the changed lives of the disciples; (2) the conversion of Saul of Tarsus; (3) the rapid spread of Christianity.

The changed lives of the disciples. The changed lives of the disciples give an indirect testimony to Christ's resurrection. When Jesus was betrayed, the Bible says his disciples scattered. "Then all the disciples forsook Him and fled" (Matt. 26:56).

Simon Peter, who had promised to die for Jesus, denied that he even knew him. "Now Peter sat outside in the courtyard. And a servant girl came to him, saying, 'You also were with Jesus of Galilee.' But he denied it before them all, saying, 'I do not know what you are saying.' . . . And after a while those who stood by came to him and said to Peter, 'Surely you also are one of them, because your speech betrays you.' Then he began to curse and swear, saying, 'I do not know the Man!' " (Matt. 26:69, 70, 73, 74).

At his crucifixion, his disciples were nowhere to be found. "But all His acquaintances, and the women who followed Him from Galilee, stood at a distance, watching these things" (Luke 23:49).

The picture we get of the disciples at the time of Jesus' trial and death is a frightened band of individuals who denied their master and went into hiding.

Some fifty days later, however, we find these same disciples standing up bravely in the city of Jerusalem, proclaiming that Christ has risen from the dead (Acts 2).

Soon thereafter this boldness of the disciples caused the religious leaders to arrest them. "Now as they spoke to the people, the priests, the captain of the temple, and the Sadducees came upon them, being greatly disturbed that they taught the people and preached in Jesus the resurrection from the dead. And they laid hands on them, and put them in custody until the next day" (Acts 4:1-3).

The religious leaders resorted to threats. " 'But so that it spreads no further among the people, let us severely threaten them, that from now on they speak to no man in this name.' And they called them and commanded them not to speak at all nor teach in the name of Jesus. But Peter and John answered and said to them, 'Whether it is right in the sight of God to listen to you more than to God, you judge. For we cannot but speak the things which we have seen and heard.' So when they had further threatened them, they let them go, finding no way of punishing them" (Acts 4:17-21).

The former cowards were now fearlessly proclaiming the resurrection of Christ. Obviously, something happened to change the lives of these men. The disciples attributed their bravery to seeing Christ risen. If Christ had not risen then some other explanation for their changed lives must be in order.

The conversion of Saul of Tarsus. A second line of indirect evidence that can be offered for the resurrection of Christ is the conversion of Saul of Tarsus to the Apostle Paul.

According to his own testimony, Saul persecuted the believers in Christ. "Indeed, I myself thought I must do many things contrary to the name of Jesus of Nazareth. This I also did in Jerusalem, and many of the saints I shut up in prison, having received authority from the chief priests; and when they were put to death, I cast my vote against them. And I punished them often in every synagogue and compelled them to blaspheme; and being exceedingly enraged against them, I persecuted them even to foreign cities" (Acts 26:9-11). Saul had believers jailed and consented to their death sentence. In doing all this, he believed he was serving God.

However, something happened to Saul to change his way of thinking. "As I journeyed to Damascus with authority and commission from the chief priests, at midday, O king, along the road I saw a light from heaven, brighter than the sun, shining around me and those who journeyed with me. And when we all had fallen to the ground I heard a voice speaking to me and saying in the Hebrew language, 'Saul, Saul, why are you persecuting Me?' . . . So I said, 'Who are you, Lord?' And He said, 'I am Jesus, whom you are persecuting. But rise and stand on your feet; for I have appeared to you for this purpose, to make you a minister and a witness both of the things which you have seen and of the things which I will yet reveal to you' " (Acts 26:12-16).

Saul obeyed the heavenly vision and became the Apostle Paul, the mighty defender of the faith. Twelve of the books of the New Testament were written by him. The greatest antagonist to the faith became its greatest champion. What was it that changed this man's life? He said it was meeting the risen Christ. His testimony is another in the line of circumstantial evidence that Christ rose from the dead.

The rapid spread of Christianity. A third line of indirect evidence, but by no means the last, is the rapid spread of Christianity. It is a historical fact that Christianity spread faster than any other religion or philosophy in the ancient world. By the early part of the fourth century, the Roman Empire became "Christianized." Something had to account for this unprecedented growth. The fact of Christianity's rapid expansion gives a further witness to the truth of its resurrection message. People embraced Christianity because they were convinced that Jesus Christ had conquered death and could offer them eternal life.

These three lines of indirect evidence—the changed lives of the disciples, the conversion of Saul of Tarsus, and the rapid spread of Christianity—are by no means the only verification that could be brought to further bolster the case for the Resurrection. But they do demonstrate that the eyewitness testimony of Scripture is supported by other evidence. The verdict is clear: Jesus did rise from the dead.

73. How Do Skeptics Explain the Resurrection?

If Jesus did not come back from the dead, as the Bible plainly says he did, then some alternative explanation must be offered to explain what happened. The problem is that other explanations take as much faith to believe as the New Testament's account of what happened. These alternative theories leave more questions unanswered than they explain. Three of the more popular explanations are: (1) the body was stolen; (2) Jesus did not really die on the cross; and (3) the disciples had hallucinations concerning Jesus.

The stolen body theory. The oldest explanation given to explain away the Resurrection is the stolen body theory. The New Testament records how it started. "Now while they were going, behold, some of the guard came into the city and reported to the chief priests all the things that had happened. When they had assembled with the elders and taken counsel, they gave a large sum of money to the soldiers, saying, 'Tell them, "His disciples came at night and stole Him away while we slept." And if this comes to the governor's ears, we will appease him and make you secure.' So they took the money and did as they were instructed; and this saying is commonly reported among the Jews until this day" (Matt. 28:11-15).

140

The Bible says this theory was conceived to explain away the fact of the Resurrection. The theory that the disciples stole the body of Jesus does not fit the evidence.

1. To begin with, the disciples would have had to get by the guards at the tomb. This theory has the guard members conveniently asleep. The disciples would have had to move the large stone away from the tomb without waking any of the guard members.

2. Assuming the disciples could have stolen the body, another set of questions arise. What motivated them to do it? By proclaiming Christ had risen, they subjected themselves to beatings and jail. They eventually died for their testimony. If they had stolen the body, they would have been liars as well as thieves. They would not only have lied for the cause, they would have died for their lie. What advantage would there have been in doing this?

3. Furthermore, these are the same disciples who gave us the New Testament. They reported that Jesus was sinless. He never lied: he always told the truth. Yet this theory wants people to believe that his disciples, while spreading the message of Jesus, lied and continued to lie about the most important event in his life. On the one hand they proclaimed to the world the story of the most perfect man who had ever lived. On the other hand, according to the stolen body theory, they pulled off this gigantic deception. This inconsistency does not make sense and is not supported by the evidence.

4. None of the disciples ever denied the Resurrection. If Jesus had not risen, one would have expected the eventual confession of some of them. But they all went to their deaths proclaiming Christ had risen. Thus the theory that Jesus' disciples stole his body is not very convincing.

Jesus never died on the cross. Another inadequate theory claims that Jesus never died on the cross. This theory has been posed in various forms, but it basically teaches that Jesus was resuscitated rather than being resurrected. According to this theory, when he appeared to his disciples it was as one who had not died, not as one who had conquered death. As with the stolen body theory, this explanation is filled with problems.

1. The eyewitnesses testified that Jesus had died. "When they came to Jesus and saw that he was already dead, they did not break his legs. But one of the soldiers pierced his side with a spear, and immediately blood and water came out. And he who has seen has testified, and his testimony is true; and he knows that he is telling the truth, so that you may believe" (John 19:33-35). Blood and water coming out separately is a medical testimony that Jesus was dead. This occurs when the heart stops beating. Furthermore, the soldiers did not break his legs because they could tell that he was already dead.

2. If it were only a resuscitation, not a resurrection, that would involve Jesus in the deception. As previously mentioned, there is nothing in the life of Jesus to even remotely suggest he did anything wrong. This theory would make him history's greatest deceiver.

There is no evidence to suggest this theory is true. It is only a concoction in the minds of those who refuse to believe the facts.

The disciples had hallucinations. This theory says that the disciples had visions or hallucinations. They are supposed to have seen someone or something that was not real—not Jesus. As with all other theories about the Resurrection, this one makes no adequate explanation of the Resurrection events recorded in the New Testament.

1. Hallucinations are defined as "unfounded or mistaken impressions experienced by individuals." Hallucinations are not collective or group experiences. The New Testament records, however, that one of the appearances of Jesus was to over five hundred people at the same time. Five hundred people at one time do not have the same hallucination.

Moreover, the New Testament says that Jesus appeared over a forty-day period many times to many different people. Then he stopped appearing. This does not fit the nature of hallucinations. They do not tend to stop suddenly for the troubled, confused person.

2. This alleged hallucination talked with the disciples for long periods of time as well as ate with them. It is hard to conceive that eleven disciples only imagined all this.

3. If Christ's appearances were only hallucinations, then the body of Jesus would have still been in the tomb. Why wasn't it produced? This would have stopped any proclamation of the Resurrection.

When one considers the alternative explanations that have been given to the resurrection story, one thing becomes clear: It takes more faith to believe in the alternative theories than it does to believe in the New Testament account. The evidence speaks loud and clear and the lack of a sound alternative explanation only supports the New Testament's claim that Jesus Christ rose from the dead.

74. Did Jesus Appear Only to Believers after His Resurrection?

One of the objections often heard about Jesus' resurrection is that he appeared only to believers. The argument goes like this: If Jesus really wanted to show the world he had risen from the dead, he would have appeared to unbelievers rather than only to believers, those already convinced about who he was. Supposedly, since his disciples were already committed to him, it would be easy to convince them he had risen from the dead. The Bible, however, gives a different story. Rather than being naive and easily convinced, we find the disciples were slow and careful to evaluate the evidence before they believed. Furthermore, Jesus did appear to unbelievers after his resurrection.

The first account we have of the disciples after Jesus'

resurrection finds them not expecting a resurrection. When the women returned to them after visiting the empty tomb, the disciples rejected their testimony. "And their words seemed to them like idle tales, and they did not believe them" (Luke 24:11). This makes the disciples the first unbelievers in the Resurrection. They did not expect Jesus to come back from the dead and, when they were first told he was alive, they did not believe.

The disciples did not believe until Jesus appeared to them. But doubting Thomas was not with them and he would not believe until he had seen Jesus himself. "Unless I see in His hands the print of the nails, and put my finger into the print of the nails, and put my hand into His side, I will not believe" (John 20:25). Thomas, like the other disciples, demanded evidence that Jesus had risen. Jesus soon appeared to Thomas and answered his doubts.

At one of his appearances, Jesus rebuked his disciples because of their prior unbelief. "Afterward He appeared to the eleven as they sat at the table; and He rebuked their unbelief and hardness of heart, because they did not believe those who had seen Him after He had risen" (Mark 16:14).

It is obvious that Jesus' disciples were not quick to believe the resurrection reports. They should have believed them because Jesus had predicted his resurrection. Because they did not, they were rebuked by Jesus.

When the disciples met with Jesus on another occasion, on a mountain in Galilee, there were still doubts in some of their minds. "And when they saw Him, they worshiped Him; but some doubted" (Matt. 28:17). The Resurrection was such a miraculous occurrence that it took a while for some of them to accept it. All of the eleven apostles, however, became convinced that Jesus had risen. "To whom He also presented Himself alive after His suffering by many infallible proofs, being seen by them during forty days" (Acts 1:3). Thus the testimony of the disciples has considerable weight, given the fact they were not expecting him to rise and afterward were slow to believe.

There was another person Jesus appeared to who had never believed in him—Saul of Tarsus. Saul, according to his own testimony, persecuted Christians. "Indeed, I myself thought I must do many things contrary to the name of Jesus of Nazareth" (Acts 26:9). Saul put Christians in jail and gave consent to their deaths.

But the Bible records that Jesus appeared to unbelieving Saul on the Damascus road. "So I said, 'Who are You, Lord?' And He said, 'I am Jesus, whom you are persecuting' " (Acts 26:15). This appearance of Jesus caused Saul to believe and to follow him as a disciple.

Therefore, when we look at the New Testament picture we do not find gullible believers easily accepting the resurrection of Jesus. Rather, we find people believing Jesus rose from the dead only after they had carefully considered the evidence.

75. What Form Did Jesus Take at His Resurrection?

It is very important to understand the form that the resurrected Jesus took upon himself, for the Scriptures teach that when we are resurrected we shall have a form similar to his. "Beloved, now we are children of God; and it has not yet been revealed what we shall be, but we know that when He is revealed, we shall be like Him, for we shall see Him as He is" (1 John 3:2).

There are some who believe that Jesus did not have a body upon his resurrection but was only a spirit. However, the Scripture is very clear on the issue; the resurrection of Jesus was in bodily form.

Early in his ministry, Jesus predicted his resurrection: " 'Destroy this temple, and in three days I will raise it up.' Then the Jews said, 'It has taken forty-six years to build this temple, and will You raise it up in three days?' But He was speaking of the temple of His body. Therefore, when he had risen from the dead, His disciples remembered that He had said this to them" (John 2:19-22). The Scripture is clear that it was the body of Jesus that was to be resurrected.

The idea that Jesus was some disembodied spirit was refuted by him when he appeared to his disciples after his death.

Jesus talked and ate with his disciples. Luke records the following episode: "Now as they said these things, Jesus Himself stood in the midst of them, and said to them, 'Peace to you.' But they were terrified and frightened, and supposed they had seen a spirit. And He said to them, 'Why are you troubled? And why do doubts arise in your hearts? Behold My hands and My feet, that it is I Myself. Handle Me and see, for a spirit does not have flesh and bones as you see I have.' When He had said this, He showed them his hands and His feet. But while they still did not believe for joy, and marveled, He said to them, 'Have you any food here?' So they gave Him a piece of a broiled fish and some honeycomb. And He took it and ate in their presence" (Luke 24:36-43).

Clearly Jesus dispelled any doubt as to whether or not he had a body. He not only appeared to his disciples and challenged them to handle him and see, he also ate food in their presence, showing that indeed his resurrection was bodily.

Jesus showed his disciples the scars of his crucifixion. Jesus appeared to the disciples in the upper room but Thomas was not among them. Thomas told the other disciples that he would not believe in the Resurrection until he could see Jesus with his own eyes and touch him. The Gospel of John records what happened after that. "Jesus came, the doors being shut, and stood in their midst, and said, 'Peace to you!' Then He said to Thomas, 'Reach your finger here, and look at My hands; and reach your hand here, and put it into My side. Do not be unbelieving, but believing.' And Thomas answered and said to Him, 'My Lord and My God!' " (John 20:26-28).

On this occasion Thomas challenged Jesus to see if he were indeed real. The doubter immediately realized that Jesus had come back from the dead in a resurrected body.

From these accounts we can see that Jesus' resurrection was bodily:

1. His testimony. He made it clear that he was not a disembodied spirit.
2. He did things only a person having a body can do. He walked. He showed them the prints of the crucifixion in his body. On the other occasions the Scripture said he breathed (John 20:22) and ate (Luke 24:41-43). All of these acts were possible because Jesus had a body.

The body he possessed, however, though like his pre-resurrection body, was in some aspects different. He could suddenly appear and disappear. In the locked upper room, Jesus suddenly appeared in the midst of his disciples. His new body had abilities the previous one either did not have or did not demonstrate. But whatever the case may be, the form Jesus took upon himself at his resurrection was a body.

76. Can Christianity Be Meaningful without the Resurrection of Christ?

If Jesus did not come back from the dead, then can Christianity have any meaning for mankind? There are those who say that even without the Resurrection, Christianity has significance. They hold that the teachings of love and Christ's example in giving of himself provide ethical guidelines for humanity. The Bible, however, testifies that this is not the case. Without the Resurrection there is no meaningful Christianity.

The Apostle Paul made the importance of the Resurrection to the Christian faith clear when he wrote, "And if Christ is not risen, then our preaching is vain and your faith is also vain. Yes, and we are found false witnesses of God, because we have testified of God that He raised up Christ, whom He did not raise up. . . . And if Christ is not risen, your faith is futile; you are still in your sins! Then also those who have fallen asleep in Christ have perished. If in this life only we have hope in Christ, we are of all men the most pitiable" (1 Cor. 15:14, 15, 17-19).

Notice how clearly Paul stated the matter—no resurrection, no Christianity. If Christ has not risen then:

1. Preaching is empty and so is anyone's faith because the object of our faith, Christ, is not who he said he was.
2. The apostles are liars for testifying to a resurrection that did not occur.
3. No forgiveness has been granted for anybody's sin.
4. Those who have died have perished; they have no hope.
5. If Christ offers us hope only in this life, then we are in a pitiable condition.

Therefore, contrary to what some people contend, without the Resurrection Christianity has no meaning, for its founder would be a liar and a failure and its followers men and women who have no hope. Thus the importance of the Resurrection to Christianity cannot be overestimated.

77. What Does Jesus' Resurrection Mean to the Individual?

If you grant the fact that Jesus rose from the dead, the question is asked, "So what?" What did it accomplish? What does the Resurrection mean to me and the way I live my life?

The Bible teaches that Christ's resurrection provides many things for those who believe in him.

Eternal life. If a person believes in Jesus Christ, then one of the provisions is life everlasting. Jesus said, "Because I live, you will live also" (John 14:19). This everlasting life is based upon his resurrection. "I am the resurrection and the life. He who believes in Me, though he may die, he shall live" (John 11:25). Thus the Resurrection secured eternal life for the believer.

Hope. Because Christ has risen from the dead and granted eternal life to those who put their trust in him, there is hope for the future. Our earthly life is not all that there is for there is another existence beyond the grave. It has been said that man can live eight minutes without air, three days without water, and about thirty days without food, but man cannot live one second without hope. We all need to hope for something better, and the resurrection of Christ provides the basis for that hope.

Christ's resurrection is the first in a long line of resurrections of those who believe upon him. "But now Christ is risen from the dead, and has become the firstfruits of those who have fallen asleep" (1 Cor. 15:20). The realization of this truth provides comfort to the believer. After writing to the church at Thessalonica on the matter of the resurrection of Christ and the eventual resurrection of the believer, the Apostle Paul exhorted the church to "comfort one another with these words" (1 Thess. 4:18). The knowledge that this life is not all that there is, brings comfort to the believer.

Because of this we do not fear death in the same way as unbelievers do. The Apostle Paul wrote to the Corinthian church: " 'Death is swallowed up in victory. O Death, where is your sting? O Hades, where is your victory?' The sting of death is sin, and the strength of sin is the law. But thanks be to God, who gives us the victory through our Lord Jesus Christ" (1 Cor. 15:54-57).

A satisfying life. A third benefit of the Resurrection is that it provides the believer with the basis to live a satisfying life. "And what is the exceeding greatness of His power toward us who believe, according to the working of His mighty power which He worked in Christ when He raised Him from the dead and seated Him at His right hand in the heavenly places" (Eph. 1:19, 20). The risen Christ gives the believer the power to live a life of fulfillment.

The resurrection of Christ is more than a historical event for it provides the basis of eternal life for the believer, hope for the future, and power to live life to the fullest in the present.

78. What Is the Meaning of the Ascension?

One of the most significant events in the life of Christ was his ascension into heaven. The Bible teaches that forty days after his resurrection, Jesus ascended into heaven both visibly and bodily. "Now when He had spoken these things, while they watched, He was taken up, and a cloud received Him out of their sight. And while they looked steadfastly toward heaven as He went up, behold, two men stood by them in white apparel, who also said, 'Men of Galilee, why do you stand gazing up into heaven? This same Jesus, who was taken up from you into heaven, will so come in like manner as you saw Him go into heaven' " (Acts 1:9-11). The fact of the Ascension is clearly stated.

Scriptures provide further testimony that Jesus ascended into heaven to his rightful place next to the Father. Stephen was the first believer put to death for his faith in Christ. As he was dying by stoning, he looked up into heaven and saw Jesus. "But he, being full of the Holy Spirit, gazed into heaven and saw the glory of God, and Jesus standing at the right hand of God, and said, 'Look! I see the heavens opened and the Son of Man standing at the right hand of God!' " (Acts 7:55, 56). Stephen saw Jesus at the right hand (place of authority) of God the Father. This testified that Jesus ascended and remained in heaven.

But what does all this signify? First, the Ascension meant the end of the earthly ministry of Christ. The last act he performed before taking his place once again in heaven was the Ascension. It was the culmination of his first coming.

It was also Jesus' return to the place of his former residence and, again, taking hold of what was rightfully his. During his time on earth, Jesus had certain self-imposed limitations. For example, he limited himself to being at only one particular place at a time. Once he ascended to the Father in heaven these limitations were no longer in force. He is now the risen Lord, awaiting the time when he will return and claim what is rightfully his.

The fact that Jesus ascended into heaven *and* remained there is also of great significance. God the Father received Jesus back into his presence. This gave evidence to the fact that Jesus' earthly ministry was acceptable. The Scripture records that the work of Jesus had been finished, and finished in a satisfactory manner. "Now this is the main point of the things we are saying: We have such a High Priest, who is seated at the right hand of the throne of the Majesty in the heavens, a Minister of the sanctuary and of the true tabernacle which the Lord erected, and not man" (Heb. 8:1, 2). All that Jesus had set out to do had been accomplished. The fact that he ascended into heaven and remained alongside the Father testifies to the fact that he had completed his mission in a satisfactory manner.

The Ascension is important for the following reasons:

1. It marked the end of Jesus' earthly ministry.
2. The Ascension allowed Jesus to return to His rightful place, next to God the Father, free from his self-imposed limitations.
3. The Ascension demonstrates our salvation has been made complete. Jesus' sacrifice for sin had been accepted as satisfactory by the Father.
4. Because Christ ascended we can pray directly to the Father through him.

Jesus Christ is now back in heaven waiting to come to earth again.

79. What Predictions Has Jesus Made That Have Been Fulfilled?

One of the ministries of Jesus was that of prophet, a spokesman for God. His prophetic ministry also included predicting specific future events. We are now in a historical position to judge whether any of these have come true or not.

Death and resurrection. Jesus predicted the manner of his death, who would put him to death, and that he would rise again. All this came to pass exactly as he predicted. "From that time Jesus began to show to His disciples that He must go to

Jerusalem, and suffer many things from the elders and chief priests and scribes, and be killed, and be raised again the third day" (Matt. 16:21).

The chief priests and the scribes were the ones who arrested him and brought him to Pilate for execution. Yet three days after his crucifixion, Jesus was alive again. The angel at his tomb on the first Easter made it clear to those who arrived: "He is not here; for He is risen, as He said" (Matt. 28:6). Jesus was able to accurately predict who would put him to death and that death would not keep him from coming back to them.

Fall of Jerusalem. Jesus also predicted that the city of Jerusalem would be destroyed. Forty years before it occurred, Jesus gave specifics as to its destruction: "For the days will come upon you when your enemies will build an embankment around you, surround you and close you in on every side, and level you, and your children within you, to the ground" (Luke 19:43, 44).

In A.D. 70, as Jesus predicted, the city of Jerusalem was surrounded and destroyed by Titus the Roman. The reason Jesus gave for the fall of the city was the peoples' rejection of him as Messiah, "because you did not know the time of your visitation" (Luke 19:44).

The destruction of the temple. Another prediction Jesus made that was literally fulfilled was the destruction of the temple in Jerusalem. Jesus specified the manner of its destruction. "Then Jesus went out and departed from the temple, and His disciples came to Him to show Him the buildings of the temple. And Jesus said to them, 'Do you not see all these things? Assuredly, I say to you, not one stone shall be left here upon another, that shall not be thrown down' " (Matt. 24:1, 2).

Jesus said that the temple would be destroyed and the stones would not be left one upon the other. This happened as he predicted. When the Romans destroyed the city in A.D. 70 they completely ravaged the temple turning over all the large stones so that not one of them was left upon another. The reason they did this was because the fire that burned the temple melted the gold from the dome and the gold seeped down in between the stones. The Roman soldiers then turned the stones over to get to the gold. In doing so they unwittingly fulfilled the prophecy of Jesus.

The story of Mary of Bethany. Jesus made a prediction that the story of Mary of Bethany would be told wherever the message of the kingdom would be preached. Mary of Bethany is the one who poured oil on the body of Jesus in anticipation of his coming death. The disciples rebuked her for wasting the oil, but Jesus said she had done a good thing. "Why do you trouble the woman? For she has done a good work for Me. Assuredly, I say to you, wherever this gospel is preached in the whole world, what this woman has done will also be told as a memorial to her" (Matt. 26:10, 13).

As he predicted, the story of Mary of Bethany and her anointing of Jesus before his death is still told today wherever the gospel is preached. The fact that you are reading about it right now continues to fulfill Jesus' prophecy.

His words would be everlasting. Another prediction of Jesus that came to pass, just as he said, concerns his words. He made the astounding prediction that "heaven and earth will pass away, but My words will by no means pass away" (Matt. 24:35).

We need to appreciate how amazing this prophecy is. Here was a man who lived in the first century A.D. and had only a small group of followers. His country was subject to Rome. Though there were no modern means of mass communication, he made the statement that his words were eternal and that they will never pass away. Although it seemed improbable at the time, it has occurred exactly as he predicted. The words of Jesus are still with us today, read and believed by untold millions. It has happened just as he said.

From the examples given, it is clear that Jesus had the ability to foretell what was going to occur in the future. Historical evidence establishes Jesus as a reliable prophet.

80. Why Did Jesus Single Out Certain Cities for Destruction?

While Jesus was on earth preaching the kingdom of God, he singled out certain cities for destruction. These were Capernaum, Bethsaida, Chorazin, and Jerusalem. Why these particular cities? Were they divinely judged as Jesus had predicted?

The reason these cities were singled out was because they witnessed more miracles of Jesus than the other cities, but their people still refused to believe. "Then He began to upbraid the cities in which most of His mighty works had been done, because they did not repent: 'Woe to you, Chorazin! Woe to you, Bethsaida! For if the mighty works which were done in you had been done in Tyre and Sidon, they would have repented long ago in sackcloth and ashes. But I say to you, it will be more tolerable for Tyre and Sidon in the day of judgment than for you. And you, Capernaum, who are exalted to heaven, will be brought down to Hades; for if the mighty works which were done in you had been done in Sodom, it would have remained until this day. But I say to you that it shall be more tolerable for the land of Sodom in the day of judgment than for you' " (Matt. 11:20-24).

We learn from this pronouncement of Jesus that God judges people according to the knowledge they receive. The examples he gave, Tyre, Sidon, and Sodom, were cities of excessive sin. The Old Testament records each of these cities were destroyed. The cities under consideration here, however, had a testimony that those other cities did not. They had the Son of God personally working signs and wonders in their presence, but they still refused to believe. Jesus said even the detestable cities of Sodom, Tyre, and Sidon would not have been that unbelieving. This is a solemn judgment by Jesus. According to

Jesus, these well-known cities of sin were not nearly as unbelieving as Capernaum, the city Jesus used as his headquarters; and Bethsaida and Chorazin, two cities that clearly saw his power.

This illustrates a truth contained in Scripture: "For everyone to whom much is given, from him much will be required; and to whom much has been committed, of him they will ask the more" (Luke 12:48). These small cities had been given the privilege of seeing Jesus the Christ at work. Their refusal to believe was a cause for divine judgment.

The city of Jerusalem was also under divine judgment. The people of Jerusalem had seen their Messiah come but they would not receive him. Jesus lamented over their refusal to accept him. "O Jerusalem, Jerusalem, the one who kills the prophets and stones those who are sent to her! How often I wanted to gather your children together, as a hen gathers her chicks under her wings, but you were not willing! See! Your house is left to you desolate; for I say to you, you shall see Me no more till you say, 'Blessed is He who comes in the name of the Lord!' " (Matt. 23:37-39). Judgment was inevitable for their unbelief.

What is the verdict of history on Jesus' predictions? History records that these cities all received a terrible judgment. Capernaum, Bethsaida, and Chorazin were destroyed and never rebuilt. Jerusalem was destroyed in A.D. 70 and was under the control of non-Jewish rulers until 1967. Jesus' predictions have been literally fulfilled. Those places where he did the greatest works received the greatest judgment because of lack of belief.

81. What Predictions of Jesus Are Yet to Be Fulfilled?

The main thing that Jesus predicted that has yet to occur is his second coming. Jesus predicted he will come again, and he gave us insight into events surrounding his return.

He will return. Jesus left no doubt that he would come again. "In My Father's house are many mansions; if it were not so, I would have told you. I go to prepare a place for you. And if I go and prepare a place for you, I will come again and receive you to Myself; that where I am, there you may be also" (John 14:2, 3). The New Testament records many promises of his second coming. The hope of believers since Christ left earth and ascended into heaven is that he will someday come again.

False Christs will appear. Before Christ's second coming many individuals will appear and claim to be Christ. They will gain a following among the people. "Take heed that no one deceives you. For many will come in My name, saying, 'I am the Christ,' and will deceive many" (Matt. 24:4, 5). History has already recorded a number of people who have claimed to be Christ and have gathered disciples. False Christs will continue to appear until he comes again.

Evil will continue. Evil will continue to reign until his return. "And you will hear of wars and rumors of wars. See that you are not troubled; for all these things must come to pass, but the end is not yet. For nation will rise against nation, and kingdom against kingdom. And there will be famines, pestilences, and earthquakes in various places" (Matt. 24:6, 7). There will be no end to sickness, poverty, or crime until he returns. Christians should do everything they can to slow down evil. But evil will not be entirely done away with until Christ returns a second time.

A future time of great trouble. Immediately before Jesus returns, the earth will experience a time of great trouble. "For then there will be great tribulation, such as has not been since the beginning of the world until this time, no, nor ever shall be" (Matt. 24:21). This time is known as the "great tribulation." It will be a time when God judges the unbelief that is on the earth. This "great tribulation" has yet to occur.

Every eye will see his second coming. Although many false Christs will arise before he returns, there will be no doubt about who the genuine Christ is. For when he comes every eye will see him. "For as the lightning comes from the east and flashes to the west, so also will the coming of the Son of Man be" (Matt. 24:27). "Behold, He is coming with clouds, and every eye will see Him" (Rev. 1:7). Because Jesus told us the nature of his second coming we can confidently say it has not occurred yet. When he does return, all the world will know.

The nations will be judged. At his second coming Christ will judge the nations. After he accomplishes this he will set up his earthly kingdom. "When the Son of Man comes in His glory, and all the holy angels with Him, then He will sit on the throne of His glory. All the nations will be gathered before Him, and He will separate them one from another, as a shepherd divides his sheep from the goats. And He will set the sheep on His right hand, but the goats on the left. Then the King will say to those on His right hand, 'Come, you blessed of My Father, inherit the kingdom prepared for you from the foundation of the world.' . . . Then He will also say to those on the left hand, 'Depart from Me, you cursed, into the everlasting fire prepared for the devil and his angels' " (Matt. 25:31-34, 41).

The dividing of the sheep and goats is the dividing of the saved and the lost. Those who have believed in him are saved from their sins and will enter into his kingdom. Those who have not believed will be judged for their unbelief and will not be allowed to enter into his kingdom. Once this judgment is concluded the kingdom rule will begin.

The following events that Jesus predicted are as yet to be fulfilled:
1. He will come again.
2. Before he returns many false Christs will appear.
3. Evil will continue until he returns.
4. The greatest period of trouble the earth will ever know will occur immediately before his coming.
5. When he returns every eye will see him.

6. Upon his return he will judge the nations.
7. After he judges the nations he will begin his kingdom rule.

These events are yet to take place, but they are as certain to occur as those predictions by Jesus which have already been fulfilled.

82. What Will Christ's Kingdom Be Like?

When Christ comes back to rule as king, his kingdom will have certain characteristics. The following are some of the many things the Scripture has to say concerning Jesus' kingdom:

He will reign on earth. There will be an actual kingdom. The kingdom will be here upon the earth. Although it is referred to as the "kingdom of heaven," it is the rule of the heavens over the earth. Christ's realm will extend throughout the earth. It will be time of prosperity and plenty. "In His days the righteous shall flourish, and abundance of peace, until the moon is no more. He shall have dominion also from sea to sea, and from the River to the ends of the earth" (Ps. 72:7, 8).

He will rule with absolute righteousness. He will reign with justice and righteousness. There will be justice for all and no corruption in the rulership. God the Father said to his Son Jesus, "Your throne, O God, is forever and ever; a scepter of righteousness is the scepter of Your Kingdom" (Heb. 1:8).

His rule will bring everlasting peace. The rule of Christ will bring peace upon the earth. Since man first rebelled against God there has been no lasting peace in the world. With Christ ruling, wars will be a thing of the past. "He shall judge between the nations, and shall rebuke many people; they shall beat their swords into plowshares, and their spears into pruning hooks; nation shall not lift up sword against nation, neither shall they learn war anymore" (Isa. 2:4).

He will rule forever. When Christ returns he will set up his kingdom on the earth for a one-thousand-year period. After his thousand-year rule there will be a final judgment of the wicked. A new heaven and new earth will be created. With everything made new, Christ will reign forever. This fulfills the promise made before Christ's birth. When the angel appeared to Mary announcing the birth of Jesus, he said, "He will be great, and will be called the Son of the Highest; and the Lord God will give Him the throne of His Father David. And He will reign over the house of Jacob forever, and of His kingdom there will be no end" (Luke 1:32, 33).

Statements in God's Word establish many specifics concerning Christ's kingdom:
1. It will be a literal earthly reign.
2. The earthly rule will last for one thousand years.
3. His rule will extend to all peoples.
4. His rule will be one of absolute justice.
5. After the thousand years there will be a final judgment of the wicked.
6. A new heaven and new earth are then created.
7. Christ will then reign forever.

It is no wonder that the Apostle Paul characterized the coming and rule of Christ as our "blessed hope."

83. Were the Two Comings of Christ Predicted?

The Old Testament prophets were given their message by God. They relayed to mankind that which God had supernaturally communicated to them. One of the central themes of the Old Testament prophets was the coming of the Messiah.

In their predictions concerning the Messiah, two aspects emerged. One depicted the Messiah as a lamb led to the slaughter. "He was oppressed and He was afflicted, yet He opened not His mouth; He was led as a lamb to the slaughter, and as a sheep before its shearers is silent, so He opened not His mouth" (Isa. 53:7).

A second major aspect referred to the Messiah as the conquering Lion of the tribe of Judah. " 'Behold, the days are coming,' says the Lord, 'that I will raise to David a Branch of righteousness; a King shall reign and prosper, and execute judgment and righteousness in the earth' " (Jer. 23:5).

These two aspects seem contradictory. On the one hand, the Messiah is the suffering servant, the lamb led to slaughter; while on the other hand, he is the conquering Lord. How can these two opposite portraits of him be reconciled?

As Simon Peter wrote, the Old Testament prophets themselves had difficulty understanding this. "Of this salvation the prophets have inquired and searched diligently, who prophesied of the grace that would come to you, searching what, or what manner of time, the Spirit of Christ who was in them was indicating when He testified beforehand the sufferings of Christ and the glories that would follow" (1 Pet. 1:10, 11).

The suffering and the glory could not be reconciled by the Old Testament prophets. What they did not fully understand was that they were predicting two comings of the Messiah. During the first coming Christ would suffer as the lamb, while with the second coming he would reign as King. This mystery was not revealed to them but to us. "To them it was revealed that, not to themselves, but to us they were ministering the things which now have been reported to you through those who have preached the gospel to you by the Holy Spirit sent from heaven—things which angels desire to look into" (1 Pet. 1:12).

Though Old Testament prophecies clearly predicted the two comings of Christ, the prophets who made those predictions did not fully understand how it would all work out. The New Testament provides the answer. Christ came the first time as the Savior. He will come the second time as the Judge and reigning King.

84. Why Must Christ Come Again?

The second coming of Jesus Christ is a central theme of the New Testament. Before Jesus left the earth, he promised to return. "If I go and prepare a place for you, I will come again and receive you to Myself; that where I am, there you may be also" (John 14:3). But why does he have to come again? Why didn't he accomplish everything the first time he came?

The Bible testifies that he accomplished that which he had set out to do. On the night of his betrayal, he prayed to his heavenly Father, saying, "I have glorified You on the earth. I have finished the work which You have given Me to do" (John 17:4). His first coming completed the mission for which he had been sent.

When Jesus came the first time, he presented himself as the promised Messiah. He displayed the proper credentials. He was born in the predicted family line and worked the miracles that the Messiah was supposed to do. But his message was rejected. His forerunner, John the Baptist, was beheaded, and the religious rulers looked for opportunities to kill him.

Because his message was rejected by the people, he promised a second coming. This second coming will not be as a lowly servant but as conquering Lord. His return to earth will put an end to evil and establish his rule based upon absolute justice. He will come again to set up that rule and fulfill those predictions that still need to be fulfilled.

The religious rulers eventually had Jesus put to death, but death could not hold him. He rose from the dead and continued to speak of his return. When his mission was finally accomplished at his first coming, he ascended into heaven where he now waits ready to come again.

Thus, Jesus carried out God's program as prescribed. In his first coming he died for the sins of the world; at his second coming he will establish his kingdom. He must come again to do this and to fulfill the remainder of the prophecies that are still outstanding—promises of our blessed hope.

85. What Did Jesus Have to Say Concerning the Fate of Israel?

Jesus appeared to the nation Israel as their long-awaited Messiah. When Israel rejected his claims, he made certain predictions concerning the fate of the nation. Those prophecies have been fulfilled as predicted.

The city of Jerusalem and its temple would be destroyed. The first thing that Jesus predicted concerning the fate of the nation Israel was that the city of Jerusalem and its temple would be destroyed. "But when you see Jerusalem surrounded by armies, then know that its desolation is near" (Luke 21:20). The armies of Titus the Roman surrounded the city of Jerusalem some forty years after this prophecy and utterly destroyed the city.

The magnificent temple was also to be destroyed. "Then Jesus went out and departed from the temple, and His disciples came to Him to show Him the buildings of the temple. And Jesus said to them, 'Do you not see all these things? Assuredly, I say to you, not one stone shall be left here upon another, that shall not be thrown down'" (Matt. 24:1, 2). When Titus destroyed the city, the temple was also destroyed, fulfilling the prophecy of Jesus.

The land would be ruled by Gentiles. Jesus predicted that the nation Israel would be dominated for a long period of time by the Gentile (non-Jewish) peoples. When he predicted the destruction of the city of Jerusalem and of the temple he made clear the fate that awaited them. "And they will fall by the edge of the sword, and be led away captive into all nations. And Jerusalem will be trampled by Gentiles until the times of the Gentiles are fulfilled" (Luke 21:24). This occurred as he predicted. The city and temple were destroyed and the people were scattered. The land remained under Gentile domination for two thousand years. Except for a few short years in the second century the Jews had no rule over Jerusalem until 1967. The prediction that the nation would be subject to Gentile rule has been literally fulfilled.

The Jewish people would be persecuted. Jesus also predicted that the race would be persecuted. "Daughters of Jersualem, do not weep for Me, but weep for yourselves and for your children. For indeed the days are coming in which they will say, 'Blessed are the barren, the wombs that never bore, and the breasts that never nursed!' Then they will begin 'to say to the mountains, "Fall on us!" and to the hills, "Cover us!" ' " (Luke 23:28-30).

History records that the Jewish people have gone through terrible persecution as Jesus predicted. From the ghettos of the Middle Ages to the holocaust of World War II, the Jews have been a persecuted race.

Though persecuted, the nation would survive. Though scattered and persecuted, Jesus also predicted the Jewish people would not perish. The greatest trouble for the nation is still future, but Jesus made it clear they will still survive. "And unless those days were shortened, no flesh would be saved; but for the elect's sake those days will be shortened" (Matt. 24:22).

Jesus' predictions concerning the nation Israel foretold that:
1. The city and temple would be destroyed.
2. The land would be dominated by Gentile nations.
3. The people would receive terrible persecution.
4. Though persecuted, the nation would survive.

These prophecies of Jesus and their fulfillment demonstrate that Jesus is a trustworthy prophet. All of his predictions regarding the fate of Israel have come true.

86. What Is Jesus' Ministry Today?

The New Testament records that Jesus ascended into heaven after his resurrection. Now that he is back with the Father in heaven, what is his present ministry?

The ministry of Jesus has three aspects. At his first coming he functioned as a prophet, one who represented God to the people. At his second coming Jesus will reign as King. Presently he functions as a priest, one who is the people's representative to God.

The Bible speaks of Jesus as being our great high priest. As our high priest, he is representing those who believe to the Father. He is the Mediator, the go-between. "For there is one God and one Mediator between God and men, the Man Christ Jesus" (1 Tim. 2:5). "For Christ has not entered the holy places made with hands, which are copies of the true, but into heaven itself, now to appear in the presence of God for us" (Heb. 9:24). Jesus speaks to the Father on behalf of believers.

The reason we need a high priest is because we cannot approach God on our own behalf. God's perfect nature cannot be approached by sinful man. "Who alone has immortality, dwelling in unapproachable light, whom no man has seen or can see" (1 Tim. 6:16). When we sin we need someone to plead the case to the Father on our behalf. We cannot do it ourselves. This is what Christ does for us. "My little children, these things I write to you, that you may not sin. And if anyone sins, we have an Advocate with the Father, Jesus Christ the righteous" (1 John 2:1). The Bible paints the picture of Christ in heaven pleading the case of the believers to the Father. When the Father forgives us of our sins it is because of the mediation of Christ.

There is another purpose for him being with the Father and that is to relate our prayers. The reason God the Father hears our prayers is because of the Son. He is our access to the Father. Without him our prayers would not be heard.

Furthermore, as long as believers are in the world, Jesus will intercede on their behalf. "Therefore He is also able to save to the uttermost those who come to God through Him, since He ever lives to make intercession for them" (Heb. 7:25). He is there as long as we need him in that particular ministry.

Therefore, the Scripture says that Christ is presently in heaven:

1. He speaks to God on our behalf. Apart from him we would have no spokesman.
2. His interceding allows our prayers to be answered and our sins forgiven.

3. His ministry will continue on our behalf as long as it is necessary.

Whatever needs we might have are related to the Father by the high priestly ministry of Jesus. This is what he is presently doing on our behalf.

87. How Does Jesus Serve as a Priest?

The ministry of Jesus as our High Priest, the one who represents the people before God, is depicted in the Scriptures as being superior to the priests of Israel. Anything that the priests could achieve is performed infinitely better by Jesus Christ, the Son of God.

Heavenly priesthood. An obvious difference between the priesthood of Jesus and all the previous priests is that he performs his priestly duties in a heavenly building while they performed theirs in an earthly building. The Jewish priesthood which started with Aaron, the brother of Moses, began well over a thousand years before the time of Christ. The Jewish priests all performed their duties in an earthly structure—the tabernacle in the wilderness or the temple in Jerusalem. Jesus acts as our High Priest in a heavenly sanctuary. Immediately after his ascension into heaven Jesus became our spokesman with the Father where he now makes intercession on our behalf. His priesthood is superior to all the earthly priests who went before him because of the place where his duties are performed.

Spiritual sanctuary. Furthermore, the duties of Jesus as our priest are performed in a spiritual sanctuary. In Exodus 25:40, God gave Moses detailed instructions on the building of the tabernacle and its furniture, patterned after one made in heaven. The ancient priests ministered in the earthly physical building while Jesus ministers in the spiritual building. The one which the earthly sanctuary speaks of, the heavenly sanctuary, is superior to the earthly one. Therefore, not only the place (heaven) he ministers in is superior, the structure in heaven is superior to the ones upon the earth.

Eternal priest. Jesus' priesthood is far superior to the earthly priests in the fact that they all grew old and died while he lives eternally. The Old Testament priests, who were all mortal men, had to die and transfer their priesthood to the next generation. Jesus, the Eternal Priest, does not have to do this for he is forevermore alive and a permanent priest. "Therefore He is also able to save to the uttermost those who come to God through Him, since He ever lives to make intercession for them" (Heb. 7:25).

A sinless priest. Another problem with the earthly priests was that they were as sinful as those they represented. Not only did they bring sin-offerings for the people, they had to bring sin-offerings for themselves as well. On the day of atonement, Yom Kippur, the high priest had to go twice into the holy of holies; the first time to present a sin-offering for himself before he could enter a second time as a representative of the people. What a contrast to Christ who was without sin. He has never had to bring a sin offering on his own behalf. The Scriptures speak of him in this manner: "For such a High Priest was fitting for us, who is holy, harmless, undefiled, separate from sinners, and has become higher than the heavens" (Heb. 7:26).

Jesus stands sinless before the Father. Because he withstood all temptation, he can effectively intercede to God on our behalf in a vastly superior fashion to those earthly priests who were as sinful as those they represented.

Jesus sacrificed himself. The priesthood of Jesus is superior in another way. The sacrifice he made for sin was not that of an animal—he sacrificed himself. The animals were brought to the altar as unwilling victims but Jesus went to the cross as a willing sacrifice. "Therefore My Father loves Me, because I lay down My life that I may take it again. No one takes it from Me, but I lay it down of Myself. I have power to lay it down, and I have power to take it again. This command I have received from My Father" (John 10:17, 18). The sacrifice of Jesus was superior to those animal sacrifices performed by the priests because his sacrifice was perfect and satisfactory to God for the punishment of sin.

No more sacrifices necessary. Because Jesus was the perfect sacrifice the need for the offering of animals is now finished. Consequently there is no longer the need for the priests to offer sacrifices of this type. Jesus fulfilled this need by offering himself once and for all. The earthly priests had to repeat the animal sacrifices time and time again, but Jesus' one offering of himself ended that need. Furthermore, the Levitical priests stood when they discharged their duties, but the writer to the Hebrews says that after Jesus offered his single sacrifice for our sins he "sat down at the right hand of the Majesty on high" (Heb. 1:3). The work of the priests was never finished but Jesus' one sacrifice was complete, ending all need for further sacrifice.

Jesus' priesthood is superior to the earthly priests in the following ways:
1. His duties are performed in heaven.
2. They take place in a spiritual building.
3. The duties are performed by an eternal, sinless priest.
4. This sinless priest offered himself as a once-for-all sacrifice for sin, ending the need of the Levitical, earthly priesthood.

Conclusion to Part III

From the New Testament we can say the following things about the life and ministry of Jesus:
1. *Jesus came to earth to reveal God to mankind.*
2. *His coming was foretold by the Old Testament prophets.*
3. *Jesus preached the message of the kingdom of God.*
4. *He performed miracles to verify his message.*
5. *His kingdom was rejected by the majority of the people.*
6. *He predicted his betrayal, death and resurrection.*

7. *Jesus died on the cross for the sins of the world.*
8. *Three days after his death, Jesus rose again as he had predicted.*
9. *He appeared to many different people during a forty-day period after his resurrection.*
10. *After the forty-day period Jesus ascended into heaven.*
11. *His death on the cross means the penalty for mankind's sin has been paid.*
12. *His resurrection demonstrates that he is the Son of God.*
13. *Jesus has promised to come again.*
14. *During the interval between his first and second coming, he has told us what to expect.*
15. *In his present ministry he is interceding before God the Father on behalf of those who believe in him.*

Part IV

Jesus: His Importance to You and Me

He who has the Son has life;
he who does not have the Son of God
does not have life.
—1 John 5:12

The unchanging Good News of Jesus' message is that God loves each individaul and he provides a way for each person to be a member of his family.

Jesus explained his part in God's plan when he told his disciples, "I am the way, the truth, and the life. No one comes to the Father except through Me" (John 14:6).

And the words of the Apostle John affirm the same truth: "But as many as received Him, to them He gave the right to become children of God, even to those who believe in His name" (John 1:12).

Jesus took care to make God's love real to those who listened to his teachings by telling stories like the parables of the Prodigal Son and the lost sheep. These dramatic word pictures helped the people feel God's deep sorrow for each individual who was separated from him, and to understand God's joy over each person who chooses to be a part of his family.

When Nicodemus, the Pharisee and ruler of the Jews, came to Jesus with his questions about the kingdom of God, Jesus told him of God's love and his plan that makes it possible for a person to be with God forever. Jesus told Nicodemus, "As Moses lifted up the serpent in the wilderness, even so must the Son of Man be lifted up, that whoever believes in Him should not perish but have eternal life. For God so loved the world that He gave His only begotten Son, that whoever believes in Him should not perish but have everlasting life" (John 3:14-16).

Jesus still speaks. In today's fast-moving world of technology, political tensions, and complicated life-styles, God's love and Christ's invitation to each person is the same: "As the Father loved Me, I also have loved you; abide in My love" (John 15:9). "Come to Me, all you who labor and are heavy laden, and I will give you rest . . . for your souls" (Matt. 11:28, 29).

88. Did Jesus Claim to Be the Only Way by Which a Person Could Know God?

When Jesus came to earth he made a variety of claims about himself. One thing that he claimed was that he himself was the only way through which a person could have a relationship with the one true God. There are many who do not like this assertion because it seems narrow-minded. Others try to deny that Jesus said or meant this. But the record is clear and, whether a person likes it or not, Jesus made the colossal claim that nobody could know the living God except by means of him.

Jesus told the people of his day, "For if you do not believe that I am He, you will die in your sins" (John 8:24).

To those in the upper room he said, "I am the way, the truth, and the life. No one comes to the Father except through Me" (John 14:6).

At another time he said, "Most assuredly, I say to you, he who hears My word and believes in Him who sent Me has everlasting life, and shall not come into judgment, but has passed from death into life. Most assuredly, I say to you, the hour is coming, and now is, when the dead will hear the voice of the Son of God; and those who hear will live" (John 5:24, 25).

The idea that Jesus is the only way, the final authority, was not invented by the church but is central to his purpose for coming to earth. He came to be the sacrifice—the ransom that paid for the sins of mankind. Therefore, there is no other way to reach God except through the provision made by Jesus on the cross.

Whether a person believes it or not, the record is clear. Jesus himself believed and taught that only through him could a person have his sins forgiven and come to know the one true living God.

89. What Did Jesus Mean When He Said, "You Must Be Born Again"?

In a conversation Jesus had one night with Nicodemus, a religious leader, Jesus said that anyone wanting to enter God's kingdom must be born again. "Most assuredly, I say to you, unless one is born again, he cannot see the kingdom of God" (John 3:3).

Since Jesus made being "born again" a requirement for entering the kingdom of God, it is crucial that we understand what he meant.

The term "born again" (or born from above) refers to a spiritual rebirth. When we are born into the world we are born sinners separated from God. All of us are in this category. "For all have sinned and fall short of the glory of God" (Rom. 3:23). Our spiritual condition separates us from God and, unless something is done, it will result in eternal death: "For the wages of sin is death" (Rom. 6:23).

The problem we have is that we cannot do anything about it. Our good deeds will not win us acceptance in God's kingdom. As the Bible says, "There is none righteous, no, not one" (Rom. 3:10). Only perfection can exist in God's presence and we all are far from perfect. What is our solution?

The answer is a spiritual rebirth or being "born again." This is accomplished by us placing our faith in Christ and what he has done. His death satisfied the requirements for the penalty of sin. When we place our faith in him as our Savior we become "born again." This is the only way anyone can enter God's kingdom. Thus being "born again" is necessary if we want to know God and enter into his kingdom.

90. What Does Jesus Want Me to Do?

Jesus has done all that he can do for us as individuals. He has given his life on our behalf. But what should we do?

The first thing he wants us to do is to believe. Before we do anything else we must acknowledge him as Savior. The Bible tells us how we must do that. "If you confess with your mouth the Lord Jesus and believe in your heart that God has raised Him from the dead, you will be saved. For with the heart one believes to righteousness, and with the mouth confession is made to salvation" (Rom. 10:9, 10).

Once we have acknowledged him as our Savior he also becomes our Lord. The Bible gives us commandments that we are to keep in obedience to him. For example, Jesus said, " 'You shall love the Lord your God with all your heart, with all your soul, and with all your mind.' This is the first and great commandment. And the second is like it: 'You shall love your neighbor as yourself' " (Matt. 22:37-39).

The Bible also gives us a standard of right and wrong. Scripture establishes what things please God and what things do not. When we call Jesus our Lord, then we desire to do those things which are pleasing to him. If we refuse to obey his commandments, we have no right to call him Lord. Jesus said, "But why do you call Me 'Lord, Lord,' and do not do the things which I say?" (Luke 6:46).

Since God has made us and knows what is best for us, it is only logical that we follow what he has prescribed. Failure to do what he instructs will result in our suffering the consequences. But obeying his commandments will bring us a life of fulfillment.

91. Can a Person Be Noncommittal toward Jesus?

There are those who would like to be neutral when it comes to Jesus. They do not want to follow him as Savior and Lord but they do not want to say anything against him. They want to remain noncommittal. Is this an option that is available?

A purpose of Jesus coming to earth was to give people an opportunity to decide for him or against him. "Do not think that I came to bring peace on earth. I did not come to bring peace but a sword. For I have come to 'set a man against his father, a daughter against her mother, and a daughter-in-law against her mother-in-law.' And 'a man's foes will be those of his own household' " (Matt. 10:34-36). He came in order that mankind might make a decision concerning him and the kingdom of God.

But what if someone does not wish to decide? Jesus said, "He who is not with Me is against Me" (Luke 11:23). By making no decision or putting off a decision a person is, in fact, rejecting the Savior. Until a man or woman decides to believe in Jesus he or she is rejecting him. If this rejection continues, one will have to suffer the consequences. "He who believes in the Son has everlasting life; and he who does not believe the Son shall not see life, but the wrath of God abides on him" (John 3:36).

Ignoring Jesus will not make him go away. Favor will not be gained in God's sight by refusing to oppose Jesus. Jesus urges us to believe. "For if you do not believe that I am He, you will die in your sins" (John 8:24). It is impossible to remain neutral toward Jesus.

92. What Keeps People from Believing in Jesus?

If Christianity has so much to offer, as the Bible claims, why don't more people believe? What keeps people from believing?

The Bible makes it clear that we all have a choice and that

we are free to choose Christ or free to reject him. Those who reject Christ give many different reasons why they do not believe.

Though people may have many excuses for not believing, it ultimately depends upon the person's choice. They choose not to believe. They have not allowed the truth of the message of Christ to change them. Though the Devil tries to keep people from Jesus, he cannot stop anyone from knowing God's truth if they want to. Unfortunately, the majority of humanity has not wanted to know the truth of God. Jesus predicted this would be the case. "Enter by the narrow gate; for wide is the gate and broad is the way that leads to destruction, and there are many who go in by it. Because narrow is the gate and difficult is the way which leads to life, and there are few who find it" (Matt. 7:13, 14).

Belief in Jesus boils down to a spiritual issue. The Bible says that a spiritual war is going on between God and the forces of evil. The prize is the souls of mankind. The Apostle Paul declared, "For we do not wrestle against flesh and blood, but against principalities, against powers, against the rulers of the darkness of this age, against spiritual hosts of wickedness in the heavenly places" (Eph. 6:12). The picture given is one of warfare—a war not fought on the natural level but rather in the supernatural.

According to the Bible, everyone is invited to believe the message of Jesus. Although a spiritual battle rages for the hearts and minds of men, anyone who wants to know the truth of God can, for Jesus said, "And the one who comes to Me I will by no means cast out" (John 6:37). Unfortunately, those who come to him are in the minority.

93. Can Jesus Forgive Me?

There are people who do not consider coming to Jesus because they think that they have done things that are unforgivable. They assume that Jesus would not want to forgive them for the wrongs they have committed. Since human beings tend not to forgive each other when they have been wronged, some assume God is the same way. But the forgiveness that Jesus gives is unlike human forgiveness. The Bible makes it clear that no matter what anyone has done, Jesus can and will forgive.

The forgiveness offered by Jesus Christ is complete and covers all of our sins. His forgiveness is based on his sacrifice on the cross. His death made it possible for our sins to be forgiven. "For He made Him who knew no sin to be sin for us, that we might become the righteousness of God in Him" (2 Cor. 5:21). But we can experience his forgiveness only if we place our faith in him as Savior.

When that occurs, God forgives all our sins. He not only forgives our sins, he does not hold them against us. "As far as the east is from the west, so far has He removed our transgressions from us" (Ps. 103:12).

The only thing that Jesus will not forgive you for is rejecting him as Savior. If you refuse to accept what he has done for you on the cross, then you will not have forgiveness. But it is his desire that everyone come to him for forgiveness. "The Lord is not slack concerning His promise, as some count slackness, but is longsuffering toward us, not willing that any should perish but that all should come to repentance" (2 Pet. 3:9). He has made it possible that all of us can experience the complete forgiveness of God.

94. Why Would Jesus Care about Me?

A question that often arises is why Jesus would care about any one particular individual. With the billions of people in the world, why should I expect him to care about me? Though the earth is filled with countless people and their problems, the Bible says that Jesus cares about you and me and what we are experiencing.

The Bible records the magnitude of Jesus' love and care for us. "Are not two sparrows sold for a copper coin? And not one of them falls to the ground apart from your Father's will. But the very hairs of your head are all numbered. Do not fear therefore; you are of more value than many sparrows" (Matt. 10:29-31). According to Jesus, nothing happens that escapes God's notice. A sparrow cannot fall to the ground without God being aware of it. But his care for us is infinitely more than that for the sparrows. His care for us is so great that even the very hairs of our head are numbered. The message he is sending is loud and clear: We are important to God. What matters to us matters to him.

God's love for us has already been demonstrated by Jesus' death on the cross. Since he has given his life on our behalf, we should expect him to give us all the best things. "He who did not spare His own Son, but delivered Him up for us all, how shall He not with Him also freely give us all things?" (Rom. 8:32). If he has died for us, should not we expect him to have our best interests in mind?

Once we begin to realize the care that Jesus has for us as individuals, we should take the advice of the Apostle Peter: "Therefore humble yourselves under the mighty hand of God, that He may exalt you in due time, casting all your care upon Him, for He cares for you" (1 Pet. 5:6, 7).

95. What Happens When a Person Believes in Jesus?

Jesus Christ has demonstrated that he is the eternal God who became a human being. His death on the cross for the sins of the world offers deliverance from sin and its effects. Whether or not a person believes this, it is still true. Jesus Christ is the Lord of the universe. When anyone believes in Jesus as his Savior, his outlook on life takes on a new perspective—he becomes a "new creation" (2 Cor. 5:17) and life becomes more meaningful. Jesus touches us in our practical, daily living. He strikes at the very center of our existence. Belief in Jesus gives the individual identity, purpose, and destiny.

Identity. Belief in Jesus solves our identity problem. We no longer wonder who we are. We now realize that we are men and women created in the image of God. This means we have the ability to think, love, and communicate. We have the chance to know God because he has given us these abilities. We now know who we are.

Purpose. Along with identity comes a purpose for living. Instead of living life aimlessly we now know the reason we have been created—to love God and enjoy him forever. God has provided in the Bible a guide on how we are to live and what he requires of us. By believing in Jesus we now have purpose. We not only know who we are, we know why we are here.

Destiny. The final thing that belief in Jesus provides is destiny. We know that this life is not all that there is. We are beings made for eternity, and belief in Jesus allows us to spend eternity in the presence of God. Thus, the grave has no ultimate terror for us because we know there is a better existence beyond this life. Belief in Jesus gives us a destiny. We now know where we are going when we die and have a genuine hope for a better life.

96. What Are the Consequences of Rejecting Christ?

Many have the impression that Jesus only talked about the love of God and never about judgment. In no uncertain terms, however, his message included warnings of punishment for those who rejected his claims. Those who reject Christ will spend eternity separated from God.

The toughest words of judgment that are recorded in the Bible come from the lips of Jesus. He had this to say to the hypocritical religious rulers: "But woe to you, scribes and Pharisees, hypocrites! For you shut up the kingdom of heaven against men; for you neither go in yourselves, nor do you allow those who are entering to go in" (Matt. 23:13); "Serpents, brood of vipers! How can you escape the condemnation of hell?" (Matt. 23:33).

Jesus said that those who do not put their faith in him will suffer the consequences. "Therefore I said to you that you will die in your sins; for if you do not believe that I am He, you will die in your sins" (John 8:24).

When Jesus comes back to earth to judge the nations he will say to those who did not believe, "Depart from Me, you cursed, into the everlasting fire prepared for the devil and his angels" (Matt. 25:41).

From these statements we see that Jesus talked about God's punishment for those who do not believe. He said there is a place of judgment where unbelievers will be eternally separated from God. This is in contrast to those who do believe. They will be forever in God's presence and enjoy God's unending blessings.

97. How Will Those Who Believe in Christ Be Judged?

Christ paid the penalty for our sins when he died on the cross of Calvary. Those who believe in Christ will not be condemned. The Scripture says, "There is therefore now no condemnation to those who are in Christ Jesus" (Rom. 8:1).

But the Bible does speak of a time believers will appear before Christ for judgment. "For we must all appear before the judgment seat of Christ, that each one may receive the things done in the body, according to what he has done, whether good or bad" (2 Cor. 5:10).

What type of judgment will this be? At the judgment seat of Christ, salvation is not the issue. That already has been dealt with. The Bible says that when believers appear before Christ it will be for bestowing rewards rather than for condemnation for sin. Each believer will be rewarded by Christ based upon what he or she has done in this life.

The Apostle Paul wrote about the believers' reward: "For no other foundation can anyone lay than that which is laid, which is Jesus Christ. Now if anyone builds on this foundation with gold, silver, precious stones, wood, hay, straw, each one's work will become manifest; for the Day will declare it, because it will be revealed by fire; and the fire will test each one's work, of what sort it is. If anyone's work which he has built on it endures, he will receive a reward. If anyone's work is burned, he will suffer loss; but he himself will be saved, yet so as through fire" (1 Cor. 3:11-15). It is for those works that endure that the believer will be rewarded. These would be deeds done with the motivation of glorifying God rather than for self-glorification.

The judgment of believers will be one of reward, not of condemnation. As Romans 8:1 says, "There is therefore now no condemnation to those who are in Christ Jesus." The believers' sins have been forgiven because of Christ's death on the cross. When believers appear before Christ for judgment, it will be to receive rewards based on their enduring works and obedience to him.

98. Did Jesus Promise an Easier Life for Those Who Believe?

Many times people think that believing in Jesus will bring them a much easier way of life. But Jesus never promised this. The Bible says that those who trust in Jesus will not always find the going that simple.

Jesus said those who believe in him would suffer persecution. "Blessed are you when they revile and persecute you, and say all kinds of evil against you falsely for My sake. Rejoice and be exceedingly glad, for great is your reward in heaven, for so they persecuted the prophets who were before you" (Matt. 5:11, 12).

Jesus said the unbelieving world would hate believers. "If the world hates you, you know that it hated Me before it hated you. If you were of the world, the world would love its own. Yet because you are not of the world, but I chose you out of the world, therefore the world hates you" (John 15:18, 19).

The Apostle Paul wrote to Timothy, "Yes, and all who desire to live godly in Christ Jesus will suffer persecution" (2 Tim. 3:12).

Thus when one believes in Jesus there will be a certain amount of hatred and persecution. This is because the believer is taking a stand for the truth of God, and the unbelieving world does not love God's truth. Jesus said, "And this is the condemnation, that the light has come into the world, and men loved darkness rather than light, because their deeds were evil" (John 3:19). Consequently, those who believe in Jesus are going to fight a spiritual battle. The life of the Christian will not always be easy.

99. What Did Jesus Mean When He Said We Are to "Deny Ourselves" to Follow Him?

Jesus gave a variety of instructions to those who desire to follow him. One of the things he commanded was that his followers "deny themselves." Jesus said, "If anyone desires to come after Me, let him deny himself, and take up his cross, and follow Me" (Matt. 16:24). What did he mean by this?

The idea behind "denying oneself" does not refer to abstinence from the good things in life that God has given to us. We can still enjoy the things that he has created for our benefit. Neither does it refer to punishing ourselves in order to obtain some favor with God. What we are to deny is our self-centeredness. When we follow Christ, he becomes our primary concern and our selfish wishes become secondary. We are to acknowledge him as the Lord of our lives in all that we say and do. By doing this we deny our own self-interests.

It is to our advantage to do this. God, as Creator, has made us special. We are all different and have different needs, and only he knows what will be ultimately fulfilling to us. That which might be beneficial to someone else may not necessarily be the best for us. Therefore, when we deny self we give him the opportunity to fill the needs that we have. Denial of one's self gives God a chance to work in our lives.

Denial of one's self not only benefits us, it benefits others. When we allow Christ to guide our lives, we affect others in a positive way. Jesus' life of self-denial produced blessing for others. In the same way, we will benefit others if we follow his example. Jesus said that believers are the light of the world. We are here on earth to be a positive testimony for God. When we deny ourselves, it testifies to the goodness of God and demonstrates our love for him. Because Christ has done so much for us we should show our love by denying ourselves and putting him first. Denying our self-centeredness is beneficial to us, to others and, more than anything else, it is pleasing to God.

100. Once a Person Believes in Jesus, What Should He or She Do?

The Bible gives many instructions for those who believe in Christ as their Savior. There are four basic things each believer should do: (1) study the Bible; (2) pray; (3) meet with other believers; and (4) tell others about Jesus.

Study the Bible. The Bible is God's Word, his communication to us. If we want to discover his promises to us and know what he requires of us, we can do so by studying the Bible. The Apostle Paul encouraged believers to give diligence to God's Word. "Be diligent to present yourself approved to God, a worker who does not need to be ashamed, rightly dividing the word of truth" (2 Tim. 2:15). Thus if a person wants to know the mind of God on some issue, he can do so by studying the Bible.

Pray. The Bible is God speaking to us; prayer is our speaking to him. Prayer is simply talking to God. There is no set formula on what one must pray, nor is there any particular position we must assume to pray. Believers have the privilege of prayer because of Christ's role as our High Priest. He is the one who speaks to God on our behalf. Thus we should pray to God the Father through his Son Jesus. Even though he knows what we need before we ask, we are urged to pray about everything, telling God our needs and thanking him for the answers.

Meet with other believers. Another thing that believers need to do is to meet together regularly. Believers in the early church met "daily with one accord in the temple . . . breaking bread from house to house" (Acts 2:46). Hebrews 10:25 tells us not to neglect our church meetings, as some do, but encourage and warn one another. Gathering together is important for the purposes of worship and instruction in God's Word. Being together with other believers also allows us to share our experiences and strengthen one another.

Tell others about Jesus. Believers are also told to tell others the Good News of Jesus. This means testifying to the claims Jesus made for himself and how he has affected their lives as individuals. Jesus has commanded believers to be his witnesses wherever they are and to "make disciples" of all nations. This is a ministry that all believers should have.

Conclusion to Part IV

Since Christ has demonstrated himself to be Savior and Lord it means the following things to the individual:

1. *Jesus claimed to be the only way by which an individual can know the one true God.*
2. *Jesus said a person must be born again to enter the kingdom of heaven.*
3. *Every person has to make a decision to believe in him or reject him.*
4. *It is impossible to be noncommittal toward Jesus.*
5. *A person who believes in Jesus will receive everlasting life.*
6. *Those who reject him will experience the judgment of God.*
7. *Jesus has shown that he cares about us in everything that we do.*
8. *He will forgive any sin that we commit.*
9. *The Bible gives instructions on how to live a life that pleases God.*

101. A Final Question

Now that we know who Jesus is and why he came to earth, there is one final question that must be asked. This question is for the reader. Have you personally made a commitment to Jesus? Do you know him as your Savior?

If you would like to know Jesus as your Savior, he has made it a very simple thing to do. The Bible says, "But as many as received Him, to them He gave the right to become children of God, even to those who believe in His name" (John 1:12). You must, by faith, receive Jesus as your Savior. As we have seen in this book, Jesus has provided an intelligent basis for faith. He is asking you to make that intelligent step of faith.

If you would like to take that step right now, I encourage you to pray: "Lord Jesus, I know that I am a sinner, I realize that I cannot know God on my own. I thank you for dying in my place. Right at this moment, the best way that I know how, I trust You as my Savior. I pray this in Jesus' name, Amen."

If you sincerely prayed that prayer then you are now a Christian! An exciting life with God awaits you. If I can be of any help to you please write to me in care of the publishers. God bless you.

Summary

Having answered questions on the life and ministry of Jesus Christ we can now conclude the following:

1. *Jesus existed.*
2. *The New Testament contains reliable information about him.*
3. *The New Testament has been transmitted accurately down through history.*
4. *Jesus has been God for all eternity.*
5. *He became a man to show us what God is like.*
6. *Jesus also came to earth to die for the sins of the world.*
7. *He died on a cross for all of our sins.*
8. *Jesus rose from the dead three days after his death. This demonstrated that he was who he claimed to be.*

9. *His sacrifice on the cross offers forgiveness of sin to all who believe in him.*
10. *Jesus claimed to be the only way by which a person could know the living God.*
11. *Those who believe in Jesus receive everlasting life.*
12. *The ones who do not believe in Jesus will be separated from God forever.*
13. *The choice of believing or not believing in Christ is up to the individual.*
14. *Once a person believes, the Bible gives him instructions on how to live.*